MODERN DANCE

MARY V

MARTHA C

CHARLES S

DORIS H

HARALD K

PAL U

HANYA A

PAUL L

HANNS HA

ARTUR M

VIRGINIA S

MERLE ARM

IGMAN

GRAHAM

WEIDMAN

UMPHREY

EUTZBERG

CA

O L M

O V E

T I N G

C H E L

E W A R T

T A G E

NEW YORK 1970

This book was compiled by Virginia Stewart. The first edition consisted of five hundred numbered copies. It was manufactured in the plant of the Will A. Kistler Company under supervision of Lynton R. Kistler, after designs by Merle Armitage. The text is set in twelve point Italian Old Style type, with chapter headings in light face Kabel. The illustrations were reproduced by photo-offset. Produced in August, 1935.

FOREWORD

During its long years in that limbo known as "out of print", this most welcome book has been quietly acquiring a uniqueness that could not have been anticipated. And this on several fronts.

For one thing, it is the first instance in which leaders of both the German and the American modern dance were persuaded to "speak their pieces" in a printed symposium. (And, parenthetically, a symposium that has not been equaled since in the unity of its excellences—its admirable compilation and, one might almost say, collation, by Virginia Stewart; the beauty of its design by Merle Armitage and of its printing by Lynton R. Kistler.)

Another aspect of its uniqueness is its providential timing. It could not have happened much earlier (August 1935) or it would have found the American dance not yet at a stage of maturity to be compared with the older manifestations in Germany. If it had come much later it would have found the German dance on the verge of decline and ultimate disintegration. In August 1934 Hitler had been proclaimed Führer.

To turn back these thirty-five years, indeed, is to evoke not only nostalgia but deeper and more penetrating sadnesses—death, demolition, disillusion. But there are brightnesses as well, and one of them constitutes the book's third and perhaps happiest claim to uniqueness. This is the statement written by Paul Love for and with Doris Humphrey (who mistrusted her own literary capacity) of her essential theory. It is inevitably dated (which is not at all the same thing as outdated), but it is nonetheless quite the best statement anywhere to be found of a specific approach to creative practice that delves all the way down to the roots of universality as no other theory has done in this country since Isadora, and in Europe since Wigman. To the sometimes visionary, sometimes mystic, most of the time only partially articulate, greatness of these older theories, there is added a clear, pragmatic, almost blunt exposition, in terms of experience, of the stuff of dancing, age-old and into perpetuity.

Thus a book that seemed good when it was new has proved to be immeasurably more valuable now that it is old. It may, indeed, have become indispensable.

JOHN MARTIN

Los Angeles
November 1969

CONTENTS

Part III—BIOGRAPHICAL SKETCHES

INTRODUCTION

After centuries of suppression by the church, domination by rigid musical forms and disregard by the general public, the dance is again coming to be recognized as a major art. It is being accepted and utilized as an exhilarating body training for modern life, as an emotional release and an enrichment of individual expression, as well as a way leading toward powerful creativeness in the modern spirit.

But unfortunately, there is still in America considerable confusion in the mind of the dance public, and even of the dancers themselves as to the technical basis of the modern dance, why the modern dance developed, and the nature of its aesthetic implications. It is the intention of the following paragraphs to attempt to answer these three questions.

WHAT IS THE TECHNICAL BASIS OF THE MODERN DANCE? In Germany, where the so-called "modern" dance first appeared, the dancers practice daily exercises to develop and perfect the body control so necessary to the creative period. These are in the form of "gymnastik." But this gymnastic is not what Americans generally associate with the word. In the new German dance school, the name of the dance work is almost invariably "tanzgymnastik," which means that the exercises are not given for the sake of bodily development alone but because they also lead to the artistic dance. The gymnastics of the daily training lesson are given with music that inspires concentrated activity with a lifted spirit. The work is strenuous and creates in the student a feeling of great physical exhilaration and emotional release.

But such work as this is only the training lesson. The students go the following hour into a class for dance work, then into classes for group dance, improvisation, composition, percussion, history of dance music, pedagogics and related subjects. Thus they are thoroughly trained as dancers or teachers. At the same time they are given the opportunity to develop their human and dance personalities by submerging their own individual experience in that of the group, by developing their rhythmic feeling and by achieving emotional release and expression through dance composition. The first principle and high purpose in the German dance is that "our innermost experiences, without being pre-arranged or studied, shall be given the opportunity for expression through movements which are free from prescribed rules and restrictions." (ALICE BLOCH: *The Art of the Body*.)

Having appeared first in Germany, the modern dance sprang up about ten years later in America. But it cannot be said that the modern American dancers began their first dance training in the new school. Those few dancers who have reached recognition in America began their training before the modern school was born or even transplanted here. Most of them started in the school of the ballet or the "natural dance." Those who believed, or unconsciously felt that they were on the wrong track broke away and started out alone to find their own true medium of expression.

That is exactly what happened in Germany about 1920. Today, in Germany, dancers and schools of the modern dance have been accepted, the schools having trained many score of dancers from the beginning of their studies. That same period of development is taking place in America now and arrival at the goal is within reach. There is no denying it. Serious young students of the *art* of the dance are turning in that direction in ever increasing numbers. And because there are less than a half dozen artist-teachers of the modern American dance, students are studying with teachers of the German dance. Thus, to sum up the question as to the technical basis of the modern dance in America, it can only be said at this stage in its development, that in many cases it is derived from the German technique, in a few instances is true "German Dance," and in still fewer instances it is a unique contribution developed by an American dancer. The latter is comparable to the non-routine, free movements of the New German dance because of the similarity of ideals.

WHY HAS THE MODERN DANCE DEVELOPED? The modern dance is the inevitable result of the tendencies of the classic and romantic traditions. Because of the artificiality of movement in the classic dance and the lack of essential form to express the spirit of the romantic, there was a positive need for a dance that has not only natural movement but also form. Hence, "the modern dance has actually arisen in fulfillment of the ideals of the romantic movement. It has set itself against the artifice of the ballet, making its chief aim the expression of an inner compulsion; but it has also seen the necessity for vital forms for this expression, and indeed, has realized the aesthetic value of form in and for itself as an adjunct to this expression. In carrying out this purpose, it has thrown aside everything that has gone before and started all over again from the beginning." (JOHN MARTIN: *The Modern Dance*.)

People found, after the world war, that they had strayed a long way from nature and from simple, intelligent living. The much maligned machine age had taken away their individuality and reduced them, to a great extent, to automatons. Nature and rhythm and soul had become empty names. On the tide of a slogan about democracy, and with a surge of pent up energy and emotions, the United States was carried into a war which gave young American manhood a complete vacation from conventional ways. They lived and fought like beasts, following commands like machines. They came home sadder and wiser, with energies dissipated, faith gone and with a sincere desire for sane living.

In Germany, then, there came the fanatical Youth Movement. Young men and women put on hiking costumes and roamed the mountains. Everyone in Germany studied gymnastics, many went further into tanzgymnastik. There was a great and perhaps profitable expenditure of youthful energy and enthusiasm. In America, the Jazz Age came into being. Young men and women put on evening clothes and went into night clubs and speakeasies where they swayed paganly to the syncopated beat of primitive melodies. There was another great expenditure of youthful energy and enthusiasm. In Germany there has been a settling down to a more normal, natural life. In America there has been a trend toward athletics and recently an interest in the dance as an art.

In both countries, just as there had been an unrelieved physical tension, there had also been a spiritual fatigue and cramping that took away freedom. And so it was discovered that rhythmic exercise, whether in the swinging step of the hikers, the measured pattern of the football formation, or the natural movement of dancing, could bring youth back to sane living with an opportunity for release and expression through free and unrestricted activity. The inherent nature of this rhythmic feeling was discovered, and though long repressed, it was capable of being drawn out and awakened.

That is the reason why the modern dance, as evolved by a few representative artists, and today is carried on by the few who have stood the test of time, has gained a great following among the youth of the Western World. And that is also the reason why the modern dance is a human means of expression far removed from the formless and the artificial.

WHAT ARE THE AESTHETIC IMPLICATIONS OF THE MODERN DANCE? Whether in Germany or America, the modern dance is an expression through an irrational medium of bodily movement of the grasped but inarticulate emotional and intellectual experiences which Man, in the whole history of his culture, has never been able to convert into words. If the spiritual content, the meaning of a dance, could be converted into words it could be better written than danced. It is the high purpose of the dance to convert these intangible mental urges, these deeply felt but inexplicable emotions, into movement.

It is this very inability to translate the meaning of dance creations into words, the very fact that the feelings aroused by these creations in the spectators are seldom identical, that give to the modern dance its greatest and strongest "raison d'etre." Movement, the substance of the dance, reveals that "inexpressible residue of emotion" (GILBERT MURRAY) which cannot be conveyed through words or pantomime.

And if the essence of this revelation of emotion through the modern dance is tragic, it is because "sorrow, being the supreme emotion of which man is capable, is at once the type and test of all great art. What the artist is always looking for is the mode of existence in which the soul and body are one and indivisible; in which the outward is expressive of the inward; in which form reveals. For truth in art is the unity of a thing with itself; the outward rendered expressive of the inward; the soul made incarnate; the body instinct with spirit. For this reason there is no truth comparable to sorrow." (OSCAR WILDE: *De Profundis.*)

Another thing not always understood is why no two dancers can or care to agree on the technical basis of the modern dance, and why no two observers can agree upon a standard of criticism applicable to all modern dancers. The reason is that the modern dance is a point of view, not a system. The foundation of the modern dance is in the modern spirit. The principle underlying this point of view is that emotional experience can express itself directly through movement. And as emotional experience varies in each individual, so will the outward expression vary. *But form, complete and adequate, must be the starting point if the modern dance as an art-form is to live.*

JOHN MARTIN admirably sums up the answers to the three questions considered when he says, "Where the classic decadence was a machine that manufactured nothing, and the romantic revolution was an attempt to manufacture something without a machine, to express something outside and above one's self, the modern dance has arisen to manufacture something with a highly perfected machine; to express only what is in and of one's own experience, transformed and lifted out of the commonplace and the personal by the very process of artistic creation, of aesthetic form."

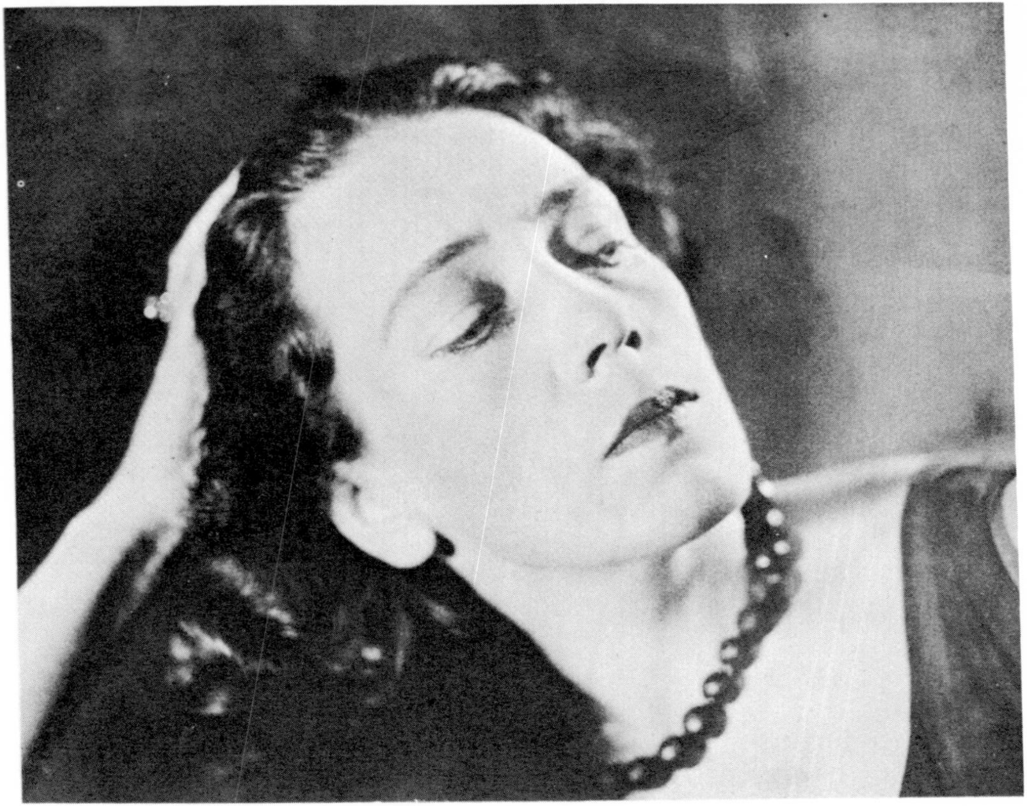

WIGMAN

GRAHAM

KREUTZBERG

GRAHAM

HASTING

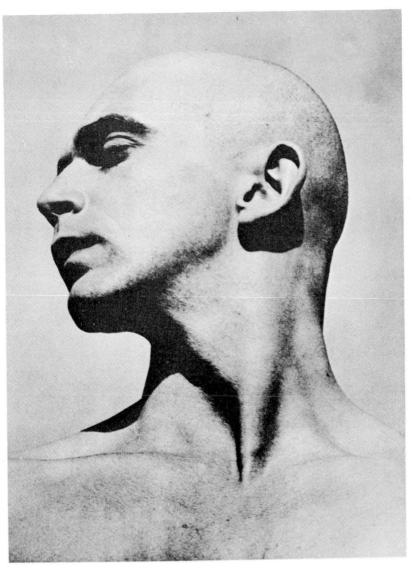

KREUTZBERG

HUMPHREY

KREUTZBERG

GRAHAM

GRAHAM

HUMPHREY AND WEIDMAN

WIGMAN

WEIDMAN

PALUCCA

WIGMAN

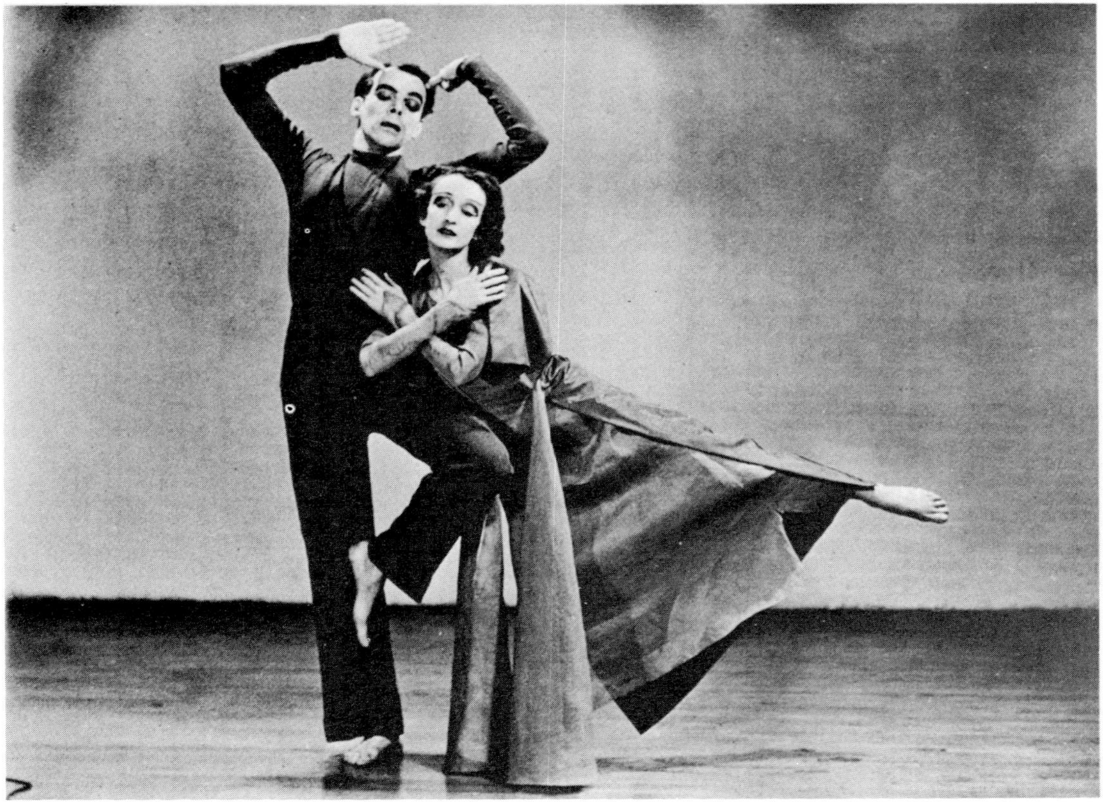

WEIDMAN AND HUMPHREY

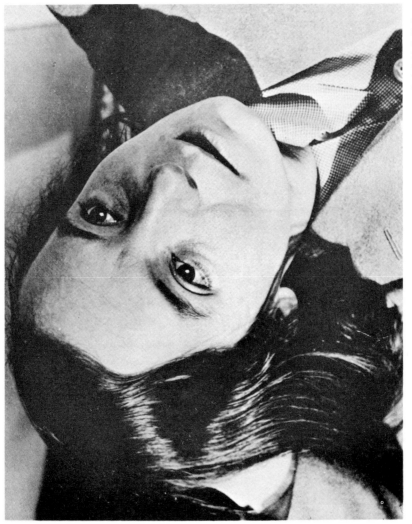

WIGMAN

HOLM

HOLM

HUMPHREY AND GROUP

PALUCCA

PART I
THE MODERN DANCE
IN
GERMANY

MICHEL

One of the most striking characteristics of the nineteenth century European was his lack of a sense of space. In other words, his consciousness of life stood in no tensive relationship to the medium in which it was lived. This was inevitably reflected in the stage dancing of the time, which became an art that placed the living body *in* space, only to demonstrate most clearly its inability to establish any relationship *with* space.

This nineteenth century stage dancing, generally known as the ballet, though danced in space, was a subtle play of the body with itself, irrespective of space. The dance did not compel, urge, elicit the gesture out of the body into space, but made it perform carefully studied movements in space. It was not an elemental force, but a refined craftsmanship.

The solo dancer was a great virtuoso displaying the brilliant technique of an instrument. Partnership did not mean the compelling expression of connection denoting bodily coalescence and space tension at one and the same time, but rather, the uniformity or complementation of skill. Group dancing was mass movement aided by decorations and light effects, which at first confused the spectator, only to delight him the more by the clearness and grace of the design that followed. It was the dividing, joining, arranging of objects in space, but not the penetration, the shaping of space itself. Group dancers were equally trained members of formally unrolling and grouping patterns. They were not the bearers of space functions, the outcome of which is mass tension driven to motion. Materially, this ballet reflected a world of faint romanticism, a fairy world, a world of unreal, idle playfulness.

Two attempts were made by the ballet to escape from formalism and to get in touch with reality. One took place at the beginning of the nineteenth century in the form of the "choreodrama" of the great Italian dancer, SALVATORE VIGANO. In consequence, however, of the early death of its ever-experimenting creator, it was never completed in practice, nor did it reach a teachable theoretic basis.

The second attempt was at the beginning of the twentieth century in the work of the Russian, MICHAEL FOKINE, of the Diaghlieff Ballets. FOKINE was already influenced by the revolutionizing ideas of ISADORA DUNCAN. But he misunderstood them. He was under the illusion that it was possible to pour new wine into old bottles, to infuse a new spirit into the technique of the classical ballet, thus converting it into a new motion language.

The new forms of movement adopted by FOKINE were governed by the rigid ballet style, though they were copied from ancient works of art or from Russian and Oriental folk dances, and by his successors from the world of work and sport, society and music hall, gymnastics and acrobatics. The Diaghlieff ballet art remained formal, remained "l'art pour l'art."

The ingenious attempts of NIJINSKY to supersede the ballet formalism never passed the stage of promising experimentation.

Dancing as an expression of experienced life was the modern conception of the art claimed and brought into being by the young twentieth century.

Where the ballet had denied reality, modern dancing affirmed it. The aim of the latter was to create from life, not from technique. The experience of the realities of life in their deepest and most intensive forms, from the direct, tangible events of the day to the mystic, ecstatic conquests of metaphysics was

4

to become the foundation and objective of dancing, as of literature, music, painting and sculpture.

The decisive problem was to bring the creative impulse, the artistic urge for expression into immediate organic connection with movement. The actual artistic question for the dancer was how to turn her dance vision into a congruent form of motion that would express that vision, and that vision only, with complete integration and perfection. Or differently stated, the question was how to induce the movement to issue, life-like, from ardent impulse. It was this question that MARY WIGMAN was the first to ask herself with unrelenting insistence.

To realize the human being as tension in space; that is, the dissolution of the dancer into swaying movement discharging tension, was the idea, the task, the aim of MARY WIGMAN. No one but a being so superbly and demoniacally possessed, so stretched between heaven and hell as was MARY WIGMAN could ever have succeeded, in the dancistic sense, in embodying human existence as tension within herself. Only such a person, perhaps, could have conceived the idea of creative dancing as the oscillation of a human being between external poles of tension, thus transplanting the dancing body from the sensually existing sphere of materialism and real space into the symbolic supersphere of tension space.

The way from conception to realization was long and hard. MARY WIGMAN achieved it with the help of RUDOLPH VON LABAN's theory. LABAN's discovery may be expressed in a few words. He recognized the legitimate connections between the structure of the human body and its capacity for direction and motion. Though different in results, the laws of movement are the same as those that govern everyday life in work, sport, dance, or gymnastics. All the

5

possibilities of direction and destination that are available to man in general, are available to the dancer. Instead of the predetermined gestures and poses of the ballet, LABAN set up the natural, dynamic urge-to-motion that impels the dancer to the space-rhythmic self-discharge as the Alpha and Omega of dancing.

From this conception of the function of the urge-to-motion, it follows that the dance movement is genuinely significant only in so far as it is an expression of the entire personality, the active inner life of the dancer. Thus this theory of the dance demands as its first principle, the self-expression of the dancer's personality.

All of the truths that LABAN disclosed have been incorporated in the work of MARY WIGMAN. When she is dancing, her torso and limbs seem to be governed by a power of nature acting after secret laws. In short, MARY WIGMAN is the first dancer who made of her body a perfect instrument of the will-to-dance. Her development could only be demonstrated exhaustively with illustrations of all of her dances and dance programs.

The products of the first great period in this development, to touch upon them briefly, were the "Evening Dances" of 1924. They formed the climax of a seven years' growth that lead through ever greater dramatic contests between the demon and the god within her. Deepest horror and highest ecstacy, unchained passions and religious pathos characterized these dances. The dancer was rent with tensions whose excessive power at first bewildered more than it seized the spectator. With the increasing diversity of movement, the mental breadth and elaboration of her dances grew. The manner in which she released her dance-tension became more and more refined, as did her art of composition, of phrasing and of gradation. A polyphony of movement gradually unfolded itself in a manner otherwise found only in authentic Asiatic dancing, as in Siam, Cambodia, or Java. She used her limbs like the varied instruments of an

6

orchestra, without their motion becoming anything but the natural flux of melody from the body-center.

At the same time, the structure of the dances became simpler, advanced on straighter lines, grew more complete. This stage of development was epitomized by the somberly tragic "Evening Dances." In them, the deeply stirred, sonorous melody of body-movement again and again would cease abruptly. A fierce, sweeping ascent would sink back repeatedly into physical suffocation, weariness, darkness. They ended, on the whole, in collapse or resignation. Such were their most striking characteristics.

At this juncture, MARY WIGMAN, tragedienne of solo dancing, may be said to have already been transformed into a dramatic dancer as far as dramatically conceived group dancing is concerned. The same urge to create that had turned her own body into a vehicle of orchestral polyphony, now realized itself in an orchestra of moving bodies. MARY WIGMAN's dance creativeness more and more insistently demanded that the polarity of space tension be made visible by a second dancer, or by a group, in addition to its manifestations by a single dancer.

MARY WIGMAN's appearance with a group for the first time in 1923 resulted in two great surprises. First, out of the mute medium of body movement, a new form of art had been created. It was a drama of motion that conveyed just as much to the spectator versed in dancing as the spoken play or musical drama could have done. To see this performance was to see the creation of drama from the spirit of dancing. Second, and still more surprising, was the perfect discipline of the dance performance as to the productiveness of the group both as individuals and as a whole. There seemed to be perfect agreement between will and technical power; in this case between the will of the leader and the power of the pupils.

7

The group was soon able to adopt spontaneously the superb style and the artistic intentions of the solo dancer, MARY WIGMAN. Single dances and group work could be brought into that close connection, that reciprocal action which marks MARY WIGMAN's art of that period. In the following years, the tragic sentiment displayed in the "Evening Dances" in the form of a direct confession, was transformed into a world of mythical apparitions in "Visions."

A crowd of unblessed, restless phantoms were now conjured up by MARY WIGMAN's dances, fantasies only known to others through tormenting dreams. She created a world of horror, peopled with sub-human beings, with specters, with creatures whose tragic craving for the bliss of being human was there given form. Behind the figures of the precious Asiatic "Zeremonielle Gestalt;" of the lucifer-like "Witch Dance;" of the bizarre "Traumgestalt," loomed the group pantomime, "Totentanz" which described the raising of the dead by their demoniacal leader into a weird existence as specters, followed by their struggle against being forced back into nothingness, only to meet their final destruction by the eerie force of the relentless demon.

A still later and very significant epoch in the history of MARY WIGMAN's work is marked by the cycle "Shifting Landscape" of 1929. It registered the repudiation of both the tragic and mythic-mimic form of the "Visions." For even in "The Face of Night" neither a specter nor a ghost was portrayed, but the vision of night itself as it came whisking in to suddenly overawe the spectator with its horrors. This night song, however, was but the dark background against which the "Shifting Landscape" of the six successive dances appeared. All of them, in the strict logic of their construction, in the perfection of their phrasing, diffuse the superpersonal atmosphere, the colorfulness and light, the temperature and odor of an enchanted landscape.

To summarize what MARY WIGMAN achieved in lyric dancing, she made equally visible by means of her own space-shaping gesture, an atmosphere of the soul or of a landscape. She strove at the same time, by working with her pupils, for dramatic collective dancing.

When MARY WIGMAN showed her first studies of "choric dancing" in a public performance in the spring of 1929, it became apparent that the ensemble art had been given new form and meaning. She displayed also, that choric movement was different in character from group dancing, and that it offered the dancistic mass innumerable new possibilities of scenic activity. To explain further, the dancing group is a personality, an acting, suffering creature assailed by dance tension which drives it to struggle with a visible (or invisible) partner. The chorus, on the contrary, is a dancistic mass. Its movements are not the expression of what it is feeling individually. It moves according to impersonal laws. It might be compared to some work of architecture come to life, moving, transforming itself from one shape to another.

Nevertheless, the real choric dancing is by no means merely a play of architectural structure formed of dancers. It claims the right to the name of dancing because, from the dancistic point of view, it is a space-shaping creation and re-creation of this form of body tension. It is not architecture for architecture's sake, but architecture which, in its incessant change, produces a spiritual atmosphere.

An opportunity for the realization of her new ideas of choric dancing seemed to offer itself to MARY WIGMAN in the choric-dramatic "Vision for Word, Dance and Light" called "Totenmal." It was composed by the Swiss poet, ALBERT TALHOFF, as a memorial to the men killed during the World War. With the aid of the town of Munich, "Totenmal" was performed in 1930.

9

The poet's intention had been to let the mourning of mothers, wives and sisters of millions of dead soldiers be expressed so strongly that they would be called back to the world of suffering by the mythical power it evoked. The stage presentation of TALHOFF's work proved that he had set himself too big a task. But that which the poet had in mind, that which had seemed impossible, was achieved through pure movement by MARY WIGMAN's art.

The deepest emotion evoked by the "Totenmal" was given expression through MARY WIGMAN's solo dancing. It was a variation of but one gesture, the movement of the arms from above slowly down and down, deeper and deeper. The monumental grandeur, the overwhelming rhythm depicted lamentation, resignation, destruction, not of a single individual, but of a whole world of women.

This dance was a prelude to MARY WIGMAN's hitherto greatest and purest creation, the dance cycle "Sacrifice." In "Shifting Landscapes," the human being was the vessel and mirror of all life's marvels. Here it stood (to use the words of German mediaeval mysticism) on God's soil, the threshold of its own return to the godhead. The title of the work, "Sacrifice," in itself seems to imply the mystic, sacramental sense of the work, the merging into the godhead. Each of these dances shows primarily, the connection between the creative man rooted in life and religious powers from another world.

Even death here becomes the bliss of returning to God. It is an impossibility to depict the powerlessness to escape the end in any more terrifying colors than by the three rushing diagonal runs that form the arch pillars of the "Dance into Death." But when, after receiving the death blow, the prostrate body rises once more, reels and dances as if it were gazing and moving into eternity, the creation seems to merge with the infinite.

Such a work could only be accomplished by a dancer whose body had become "clay in the potter's hands", had become an instrument responding in every slightest swaying phase to the dancer's will. Only so could all material rigidity of physical gesture be dissolved into nothingness, into complete transparency.

This work matured while MARY WIGMAN was preparing for her second tour through the United States. For her third tour, she devised a work of entirely different style in the group dance called "The Way." Quite indisputable about this much disputed work was the marvelous discipline of the performing group dancers.

In the beginning of 1934 MARY WIGMAN started to add to her repertoire two dances, "Dances of Women." Both of the dances showed an unexpected change in MARY WIGMAN's art. Once more she produced something absolutely new. It was no more a dancing of a human being in the charm of eerie forces, no dancing shadowed by the eminent danger of death, and no dancing in the glorifying sight of the grace of God. Now a woman was dancing who was nothing but a woman, a woman of this world, whose sorrow and whose happiness, whose life and whose fate we all share.

She combined with the new gesture of the soul a new gesture of expression. These dances were developed out of the simplest and most natural gestures. Movements so soft that they can hardly be described formed their motives. This consordino-music was true expression of the tender inward things which the "Dances of Women" wanted to say. "Farewell" was the title of the first of the two dances. The person who is left is seized by running unrest, growing into overwhelming pain. This pain is modulated and dissolved into great composure and into the consciousness of an inevitable fate. But out of this clear consciousness, the pain grows with ever increasing strength, dissolving into a sob that flashes through the whole body. The dance ends with an appealing gesture of which one does not know whether it is a beckoning, a last resigning farewell, a pining away with grief.

Totally different is the "Dance of Quiet Joy." This scherzo begins with a soft and brightly sounding swaying; it develops into a winged haste and concentrates in an immensely easy and elastic whirling dance. It is an alternate play of volatile, soaring tensions and relaxations. An admirably spiritualized and quietly shining expression of inward happiness.

MARY WIGMAN combined the new expression of the dance with the dramatic style of her earlier creations, in creating the group cycle "Dances of Women," which she produced with her third dance group at the end of 1934. Five different prominent features of the woman were made visible by these dances. The woman, chosen to fulfill the rest of her life: the bride in the "Wedding Dance." The woman as mother: "Dance of Motherhood." The charge of the woman to keep the dignity of mankind even in misery and sorrow: "Lament for the Dead." The woman announcing the secrets of life: "Dance of the Prophetess." At last the demonism: "Witches Dance."

A manifoldly varied greeting, a respectful courtesying in front of the bride is the main motive of the first part of the "Wedding Dance"; in the second part the bride joins the girls for dancing: over and over again she ranks herself into the rows of her dancing friends, over and over again she is eliminated. But she always remains the center of the dance. The bride's solemn farewell from the happiness of youth!

The "Dance of Motherhood" is a solo dance of MARY WIGMAN. A few motives are sufficient for revealing the sanctity and greatness of maternity:

the kindness willing to embrace everything with love; the humility with which the blessedness of maternal mission is carried out; the power of complete devotion and sacrifice.

The "Dance of the Prophetess" is a solo dance as well; but is accompanied by a group of six girl dancers. The dance is reminiscent of the style of "Visions." It develops in severe hieratic gestures to a great ecstacy. The prophetess sees the future; she tries to resist the horror of what she has seen; but she is crushed down. At last she goes to face the inevitable fate in a solemn and sublime dance.

The "Lament for the Dead" is a group dance of MARY WIGMAN with twelve dancers. They start moving quietly in loose groups, single or in couples or several together, each of them in her individual manner giving way to her mourning. So the expression of lamentation changes continually and grows into a perfect art of polyphonia. This polyphonia collects into a strong homophonia: all combine movements and directions to a great circle; and the motion of the circle becomes a powerful lamentation of all. Once more the polyphonia wins the upper hand: again each of them is giving way to her sorrow. But the direction of the circle remains as it was before and, as a symbol of the sorrow they all have in common, it seizes the gestures of all the dancers: they all kneel down, and overwhelmed by the greatness of the sorrow they bend flatly onto the floor. One dancer passes into the middle of the circle, kneels down gently and bows her head.

The "Witches Dance" is a burlesque play of bodies, limbs, and heads. At first a crowded, tangled heap, it starts vibrating slowly in ever increasing elastic and shaking movements, dissolves and darts out to the floor in somersaults and grotesque jumps. The mass comes in wild motion again, stiffens into a bizarre group, dissolves again, gallops into all directions, joins for a wantoning circle dance and rushes off disappearing from view. The mistress of witches entices them to come back, after a curious whirling dance. Once more the vibration and the shaking of the thronged witches. Once more a wild reeling circle dance. Then a raving whirling of all; and they rush to combine for the final group, a grotesque heap of heads and hands stretched out. The demon in the human who had worn a tragic mask in so many of MARY WIGMAN's dances now wore a comical mask, as if his dark and dangerous power had been conquered.

MARY WIGMAN is the creator of a dance education quite her own. LABAN's theories furnished certain aids for the beginning of her pedagogic work. The completed educational system is entirely hers. For her, the beginning and end of all training is the dance-urge, something unknown to the ballet. Education for dancing involves the strengthening, clarifying, and intensifying of the creative impulses, at the same time giving them expression through firm, direct, creative movements.

The skill which the dancer thus acquires is not mechanical movement-grammar, but the ability to transform each of his innumerable impulses into productive space tension that is discharged organically in the form of dancing. Thus the dance is made a function of the dancer's desire for expression. By exercising the imagination, by listening again and again to this dance-urge, by turning all its impulses into productive tension, the skill of the dancer is trained, developed, amplified. In this manner the body gets both exercise in dance performing and power in dance shaping.

Since every bodily tension points into space and at the same time expresses a relationship with it, each exercise, being a struggle of the individual with space, is an education in the first principles of the dance. By this means, the

14

dancer learns to play upon the instrument of his body as an artist, rather than as a mechanic. Thus two faculties are developed in him. First is his dance individuality. Second is his dance-type, or his ability, according to his power and disposition, to become a member of a dance community. In other words, he learns to fit himself as an instrument into a movement orchestra.

Faced by the succession of dancers MARY WIGMAN has developed, the fact is strikingly evident that they all have their individual technique. The technical power of each dancer is the function and expression of his individuality, producing movement of an unmistakably unique character. The style and compass of expression are as absolutely different as the dancers themselves. In this way they are utterly unlike the solo dancers of the old ballet, who all disposed of the same stock of movements and displayed the same technique distinguished only by a shade of personal coloring.

This difference may be well illustrated by recalling some of the best known followers of MARY WIGMAN and letting them dance past. There is the mixture of impetuous passion, soft melancholy and jubilant wantonness, of dynamic power, tender song and elastic grace of PALUCCA; the elegance and inventiveness, dramatic sensitiveness and tragic earnestness of YVONNE GEORGI. In VERA SKORONEL, who, alas, died so young, there is displayed the eerie fantasy, the restlessness, the raving of mechanical style combined with the endless striving for organic development of expression. The dances of ERICA LINDNER are reminiscent of the rustle of woods, the scent of the meadows steeped in the power and charm of old folk songs. The movements of CLARE ECKSTEIN are bizarre, bordering on the abstruse, the tragic-grotesque. Finally, there is the combination of animal savagery and lofty human deportment, the earthy fullness of life and the stern will to create represented by RUTH SOREL-

15

ABRAMOWITSCH, who was deservedly awarded the first prize at the international competition for solo dancing at Warsaw in 1933.

The best of the male dancers produced by the MARY WIGMAN school, HARALD KREUTZBERG and GEORG GROKE, confirm the educational aim of the new dance pedagogics, which is to develop dance form from the personal impulse and to bring out the greatest contrast of type as well as the contrast between male and female. And what a distinction there is between the technical power and style of these two male dancers!

HARALD KREUTZBERG represents the type of light, capriciously swaying dancer. His dancing embodies nervous sternness, revolutionary pathos, earnest grandeur. He attracts most, however, as a dancer of delicate melancholy, playful grace and volatile lightness.

GEORG GROKE's harsh, compact, dynamic manhood still develops at each performance to a new elasticity and breadth, the limits of which are not to be foreseen. In the "Josephslegende" he shows the dramatic expression of a demoniacally possessed man. In the part of Petruschka in STRAVINSKY's ballet of the same name, he thrills his audience with the power of rage increasing to raving, of ire, of bliss, of misery, of lamentation. In his peasant dancing duets with RUTH SOREL-ABRAMOWITSCH, he ripens to an inexpressible fullness of life and at the same time to a human greatness of style. This couple carries the art of duet dancing beyond the level reached by HARALD KREUTZBERG and YVONNE GEORGI.

Recently the question has been raised as to how far MARY WIGMAN's art is specifically German art. It is German in two respects. First, she has successfully fought international formalism, the so-called classic style of stage dancing that had its origin in French traditions. By her work she has proved that the classic tradition, which once claimed absolute authority, produces a style historically qualified, a style of the past, a style antagonistic to our present life. Second, by setting up dancing as the function and expression of creatively experienced life, she not only gave it the dignity that places it on a level with other arts, but also paved the way so that it might be recognized among the deepest national artistic powers. As an artist, MARY WIGMAN was enabled, through her German nature, to attain in dancing the pre-eminence held by all real German art, that of expression as opposed to form. This is accomplished, not by disdaining or destroying form, but by infusing it with life so that it dissolves into the intensity of expression. That is the deepest meaning of the development that led from "Visions" to "Sacrifice."

Yet, by deriving the form of dancing from the original urge, and thus from the nationally determined feeling of body and spirit in every individual, she is able to acquire an international circle of pupils. For the educational methods based upon this system do not imprint, either upon the foreigner or the German pupil, a preconceived and therefore unfamiliar form. On the contrary, by fostering the most intimate impulses of the dancer, she develops all his vital powers, training him to let the form radiate from these impulses. That is, in the formation of the dancer, she develops all of the powers that constitute the strength of his nationality. This is the reason why so many young dancers of all countries, and more particularly of the United States, have been trained by MARY WIGMAN without losing themselves in their model, provided, of course, that they were powerful, vital personalities.

It may be said even now that MARY WIGMAN's merits in the art of the dance are not restricted to her personal work, her solo dancing, group dancing, or her school. She has given the art a new direction, a new foundation. She is already the starting point of a new tradition, the possibilities of which cannot be foretold.

17

W I G M A N

When a dancer attempts to size up his own works, or to observe them from a critical point of view, he finds himself in a difficult position. For that to which the dance really gives utterance cannot be put into words, nor can the dancer ever separate himself from his work to the extent that he may become an objective observer. If his dance creations arise from an inner necessity, a predestination to create, then they will aim to be, and can be, nothing more than a confession of life brought into symbolic form. They will be an acceptance of, a saying "yes" to everything that is alive and that will yield life.

In performing my own dance compositions, the passionate desire arises in me at the moment of execution, to become one with these dances, to disappear in them, to live them. I am filled with gratitude when I am permitted to feel and know that through my earnest wish, through my struggles and devotion, these dances also speak to others. What they succeed in saying, however, can never be fully expressed in a title, nor even designated by a professional term. It can only be described in connection with a general consciousness of life.

In speaking of the new German dance, whose exponent I am considered in America, I do not wish to treat the theme from the point of view of my own dances and their influence. I wish, instead, to speak of the dance itself as I perceive and experience it; as I must, indeed, represent it, since I can dance in no other way.

I would like to point out one fact in advance. I acknowledge every type and form of dance, provided I feel and know that the dancer personally stands behind the finished dance creation with his whole, undivided self, that he actually and sincerely is what he dances.

Always, in every artistic field, it is only the carriers of great works of art who determine the artistic worth and the cultural meaning of a creative current. Therefore, the new German dance should be judged, not by the many small talents, the honestly enthusiastic followers nor the hangers-on, but by the work of its few truly great representatives.

Strong and convincing art has never arisen from theories. It has always grown organically. Its carriers and supporters have been those few creative natures for whom a path of work has been determined by destiny. They have had no interest in speedily changing questions of style or fancy. Their unerring intuition has realized that Today is the self-understood result of Yesterday. For them Tomorrow is just as natural a release from Today.

When seen in this light, it is clear that the new German dance is not the outcome of a preconceived program. It received its stamp from those few creative personalities who gave it unity of content and form by their relentless efforts. This battle was concerned with the essence of things; with the human being and fate, with the eternal and the fleeting. The channel leading to the source, to the primary cause of existence was freed once more. The tragic, the heroic, until then crowded out by too much playfulness, forced its way through and gave the dance new vision.

In the last analysis, nothing more happened than that the dancer rediscovered within himself the "dancing human being" and confessed his acceptance of this in the dance. It seems understandable that in doing so he renounced, yes, had to renounce a part of those traditional dance forms valid until that moment. From then on the learned form was no longer decisive for the dance as an art, but the content itself, seeking a form of expression, endeavored to create one for itself.

Since I am expected to speak of the dance as I perceive, love and understand it, I do not wish to start with art and artistic interests. I wish to speak of him on whose account art exists in this world, of him on whom art depends for sustenance, who portrays and demands art. I refer to the human being.

The human being moves in that world of existence which he can control. He knows that he enters life only once, but not from whence he came. He knows of the singleness of his going, but not whither. He wanders the path lying between birth and death subject to laws which he obeys consciously or unconsciously . . . . the laws of existence.

Before this great law all humanity is equal, equal also under the law of kind, of species. Belonging to one species creates something in common, forces common interests. Who can detach himself from this? The human being is born into the community of species, is commonly bound and socially responsible.

In the instinctive and organic life, in the mental and spiritual life of man, characteristics make themselves felt which demand communication. Man turns to man. Man needs man. Art is communication spoken by man for humanity in a language raised above the every day happening. What would be the sense of an art that robs itself of its communication and arrogantly believes that it can turn away from man?

Art grows out of the basic cause of existence. From there it draws its creative and constructive forces. From there it receives strength to renew, rejuvenate, transform itself. And there only is it imperishable, eternal.

During the process of artistic creation, man descends into the primordial elements of life. He reverts to himself to become lost in something greater than himself, in the immediate, indivisible essence of life. Like a flash, perhaps only for an instant, he is caught and galvanized by the wave of life's great current which extinguishes him in his single existence and endows him, through this experience, with the gift of participation in the All. This is the moment of grace in which man becomes a vessel ready to absorb the energies flowing into him. This is the ecstatic state which substitutes the plane of mere knowing for that of experiencing.

On this plane, schisms and doubts do not exist, nor are there problems as yet. Here the painful is not yet to be separated from the joyful. They are one, and release in man the feeling of happiness emanating from a heightened tension and intensification of his whole being. From here man, seized in his totality, strides forth on his way to the creative act.

The inner charge which man experiences demands expression. The climax of the flow of energies pulsating through him forces him to action. Just as the rhythmic force conjures up the tonal structure in the work of the musician and limits the visual inspiration of the poet to the medium of the word, so it discharges itself in the dance-inspired personality as movement. The inner agitation and mobility embodies itself and becomes visible in the spatial and rhythmic manifestations of movement.

All dance construction arises from the dance experience which the performer is destined to incarnate and which gives his creation its true stamp. The experience shapes the kernel, the basic accord of his dance existence around which all else crystallizes. Each creative person carries with him his own characteristic theme. It is waiting to be aroused through experience and completes itself during one whole creative cycle in manifold radiations, variations and transformations.

How the dance experience manifests itself to the individual may remain his own secret. The artistic achievement alone is the only valid testimony.

The image which has assumed form gives evidence of the primary vision conceived through the inner experience. That creation will ever be the most pure and forceful in its effect, in which the most minute detail speaks of the vibrating, animated unity which called forth the idea. The shape of the individual's inner experience which is carried by the elements of existence and which has passed through his total being will also have the unique, magnetic power of transmission which makes it possible to draw other persons, the participating spectators, into the magic circle of the creation.

During the last thirty years in Germany, the dance has undergone a rejuvenation. It is equivalent to a regained depth which had been lost in the course of time and which has revived this aesthetic medium. That which marks this new dance, revealing its intrinsic expression and differentiating it from other dance forms is that it reaches back to the fundament of existence as the source of all aesthetic creation and form, like any true German art. It derives its constructive forces from the dance experience which becomes in form and content, the confession of man affected in his essential being.

It was gratifying to me to learn that almost simultaneously with the dance development in Germany the dance in America ventured onto new paths. Here, too, the creations and accomplishments of the few really great dancers were instrumental in awakening and establishing my love and respect for the new American dance. Though the forms may differ, and the conceptions even oppose each other, one common link unites the new American and the new German dance. For in both, man is held sacred as the eternally old and eternally young carrier of all that lies in the realm of human expression and experience.

P A L U C C A

The artistic dance is originated through hard work. Neither unconsidered beginnings nor indistinct meditations alone are able to produce artistic dancing that may be favorably compared with other works of art. Just as painters, musicians or poets must be thoroughly acquainted with the elements of their arts, so must the dancer be the master of the instrument of his body to a superlative degree. This means that the dancer must develop all the capacities of the body, as far as they can be made the servants of the will, by the hardest labor and the strictest self-control. To a great extent, the creations of a dancer are dependent upon the fitness of his body, making it incumbent that he give it more attention than any other artist would be required to do.

So when discussing corporal technique, which is the basis of all artistic dancing, we have to lay much stress on the necessity for practice. This necessity is so great that the dancer even finds that he must force things upon his body which seem entirely out of reach. That which people seem to enjoy most in my dancing is the complete mastery of all technical elements to the point where they are performed with quite a natural air. This cannot be acquired except by making this technique second nature so that it can be easily employed in dancing without undue effort or discomfort.

Not until technical elements are mastered to such a degree, can creative work of high efficiency be attained. I know many examples of students with creative gifts who were able to produce amazing results from their initial impetus. Especially in my school, I have often observed the speed with which beginners, who were lacking in technique but driven by their enthusiasm, could force dances from their bodies that far surpassed their real capacities. The invariable consequence is a decline in this creative power when they consciously begin to develop their talents, often resulting in serious mental conflicts. The distance from normal ability to talent is rather short, but the distance from talent to final art is very long. Before the dancer comes to understand this, it causes him more bitter hours than the outsider usually imagines. It is delightful, however, to see how genuine talent becomes productive as technical abilities increase until the final results far surpass those early efforts. Only then, can creative work on a high level begin.

The principle of practice must always be of primary importance, especially for the modern dance. Its critics, without actually knowing the facts, have reproached modern dancing because they are of the general opinion that in order to produce a dance composition, it would be sufficient to have an abstract individual idea, expressed by movements and gestures. Personally, I absolutely deny that my dances can be judged by principles that do not belong to dancing itself. I feel certain that the only true dance is the one that people have danced from the oldest times. And they danced for the joy of movement itself rather than for the purpose of telling, through it, something that could be better expressed in words or music.

It stands without saying that inspiration is necessary in order to create a masterpiece of dancing. But the best inspiration passes as mere improvisation unless the dancer knows how to preserve it and to develop it into a formed and harmonious work of art. The inspiration of the creative moment must be received by the artist with gratitude in his heart for the fate that made him, rather than another, its instrument of expression. With this gift, however, comes the obligation to cultivate it, to work it into a lasting form of permanent significance. This shaping, this constantly renewed struggle with the original idea to the end that the whole dance may seem natural and perfect from its very inception is the hardest sort of toil. The dancer has to follow the same arduous course as other artists who compose a final work from many sketches.

Whether the source of inspiration is music, newly discovered movements or an idea that demands expression seems to be of little importance. My chief concern is that the final production is pure dancing, so harmonious in itself that it will enable even the simplest people to feel the elemental delight springing from formed movement. It makes me happy to find again and again that people of different ages and classes take from my dances that which they are impelled to feel according to their own dispositions.

In Germany, a country composed of so many different types, this is precisely what happens. My dancing seems to arouse similar feelings in people and to give them something for which they have felt a need. It is for this reason that I belive that the absolute dance, free from any abstract idea is the only dance for me. Then the spectator will be able to feel that which he might not be capable of feeling were he pressed in one direction by an abstract idea. This differentiation may be compared to that in symphonic music. Just as absolute music can lift people above the commonplace by the sheer force of the thing itself, so my dance endeavors to do so through harmonious movements of a dancing human body.

KREUTZBERG

A definite style of technique is implied in the vocal arts under Bel Canto. This style was founded by the early Italian school. It had its main emphasis on the beauty of tone in the cultivation of the human voice. The importance of this method had a strong influence on the development of music. We find in the musical literature of the age, a great number of works which, in order to give a complete vocal interpretation, call for a voice training in accord with Bel Canto technique.

Other methods in later times were taken into account—the development of dramatic music succeeding the Bel Canto song. The exclusive cultivation for beauty of voice turned to a factor essentially belonging to song, namely, speech in its lyrical and dramatic sphere of activity.

Now, our problem, critical thoughts on the modern dance, puts the question, "What does the concept, 'modern dance', actually represent?"—a suggestion we find in Bel Canto. "Modern dance" means for us a definite technical style in the evolution of the art of the dance.

We need further to clear up certain points concerning the general concept—*dance*, before we go into the essence and character of this modern movement.

The instrument of the dance is the human body, analogous to the human vocal organism which constitutes an instrument for song; for example, we may in song transfer the forming of resonance from the larynx to the frontal sinus. Still, certain fundamentals which are important in the treatment of the instrument, such as the technique of breathing, will not be supplanted, much less annulled, by any stylistic tendency or conformable method. Similarly there are definite principles, due to the inevitably lawful treatment of the body-instrument in dance, which are essential to this art and possess intrinsic significance. Because of this, these concepts remain untouched by any stylistic or iconoclastic imposition; they have been generally accepted and are common to the classical as well as to the modern dance.

The dance stands to music in correlation as song does to speech. Just as allowance has to be made in song for the laws of speech, so in the dance, music has to be treated to accord with inherent musical laws.

The more speech is considered a factor of secondary importance in its relationship to music, the more must its legitimate vocal laws be observed. For just as the unnatural stress on a word in song, would make it more conspicuous, so a treatment of music, contrary to its own laws would result in bringing it more to the foreground and, in that way, allow it to have too great a meaning. If for example, the original tempo of a piece of music is changed by unnatural cutting or arbitrary rhythmic shiftings, which are unscrupulously practiced with the excuse that music has but a secondary significance, it only results in over-emphasis of the music.

It would be inconceivable that we should limit ourselves to the most advantageous vowels, a, e, and o in singing, and completely relinguish all speech connection due to the accentuation of one particular vocal method, such as Bel Canto. It is also impossible, simply to renounce all music in the dance and to limit one's self to the a, e, and o of music. For instance, such as the rhythmic elements. The modern expressionistic dance has over-stressed in this particular direction. Even though this accentuation might be permissible in exceptional instances, as in a coloratura role where the essential musical emphasis would lie in the adroit rendition, or in the dance where the rhythmic element demands such a limitation, still it would, if generally practiced, be contrary to the character of dance. Music supports in a natural relationship the dance. With the exception of a few single illustrations, dance movement has been termed "dance" solely in alliance with music. A limitation to sound and percussion accompaniment is actually found only where the development of music has not gone beyond the primitivity of the exclusive use of percussion instruments. In that case, the dance accompaniment with percussion music corresponds to a regular musical accompaniment.

Without going into an extended investigation as to how far the use of costumes, either for their characterizing or aesthetic effect, is to be considered an integral factor in the realm of dance art, the inference may be drawn that the modern dance has nothing to do with body movements in freakish costumes, abstractly performed on concert stages as an accompaniment to percussion instruments. Again and again one finds the opinion advocated that these appurtenances are essential attributes of the modern dance. These stylistic and technical innovations have called forth much controversy and have been acclaimed as characteristic of the modern dance itself, instead of giving them, despite their novelty, that place which is meted out to technique and style in any art.

The modern dance is a definite stylistic phenomenon, analogous to the appearance of expressionism in painting. It has as its aim the loosening of certain technical laws in favor of more salient emotional and atmospheric communication.

The attributed confusion in the growth and projection of the modern dance is to be explained through the disparate emphasis on pure technique, due to the practice of formulated customs, which the dance, in the form of the classical ballet, had fallen. Because of the traditional limitations of the ballet, the invigorated phraseology of the contemporary dance was felt to be the introduction of an entirely new element. Here lies the main emphasis, the strength and the merit of the modern dance. Simultaneously with this invigoration, there had to be a change in the purely technical, somewhat in the sense of an extension. This metamorphosis was brought about by the reintroduction in the dance of an emphasized articulation for which, in the technique of the ballet, practically no means of presentation in bodily movement any longer existed, attributable to an always greater elimination of the representational element.

It is evident that it is very difficult to find a clear system of technique in the freedom and variety of expressive bodily movement. The speech of the body, when the definition is on the expressive side, in many cases opposes the movement which the technique of the ballet attempts to delineate. Recall the forcefully stretched position of the back in the ballet as compared with the variability in the scale of soft relaxed movements in the modern dance. The resulting difficulties were due to the simultaneous discovery of the stylistic possibilities of expression. Even until this day, no clear system has been found. Another consequence was that many laid the technique aside completely and worked only through bodily gesture. We mentioned in the beginning, the frequency of the conception, that body expression, per se, is dance. It only represents that essential, and is solely a subordinated factor in the total dance concept. This we have lately missed in the ballet.

Another difficulty is due to the dissimilarity in the types of movement in the classical ballet and the modern dance. The first excludes completely or places classical training beyond the body training of the modern school. At present the perfect execution of a large part of classical ballet movement is only possible through an uninterrupted and totally one-sided ballet training.

We proceed from the consideration that in their technical relationship, the ballet and the modern dance partly contradict each other. On the other hand, ballet technique cannot be completely excluded, since the ballet, as well as the modern dance, have in common the use of the human body as an instrument, and as a consequence a whole series of elementary dance concepts. The case lies clear that a fusion of the two must take place. It is evident this fusion may be coordinated, without detriment to execution, by combining imperfect extension with imperfect relaxation.

Such a fusion would, of course, be at the expense of the great variety of movement now attainable in the modern dance, a loss which could be accepted since the wealth of movement is limitless. In practice this path would lead to the abandonment of certain very difficult "routines" which are accomplished in the present partisan training in both factions of the dance.

Until now there has been no workable solution. We can hardly expect to discover it in one day, since it can only be accomplished through practice. Vague attempts have been made toward this fusion, but it has been difficult because many do not see clearly the necessity for the fusion of the fundamental ideas, which have been considered here. After a short while they return to the former separation which greatly retards the progress of a logical fusion. The specific danger in this delay lies in the fact that the accomplishments of the modern dance, which emphasize exclusively the expressive side of the dance, can not live. It cannot uphold its right to existence until it has classified itself into a total concept, *Dance*.

H A S T I N G

There are no two arts having a closer relationship than dancing and music. Although the musician, and especially the dancer recognize this relationship, they also see in it a serious problem. We must therefore inquire into its nature, the reason it exists and at the same time endeavor to find its solution.

The examination of mistakes often indicates what is correct, so I shall start by considering an error which often has been and still is being made. Vaguely sensing the relationship between music and the dance, the first so-called "modern" dancers misunderstood the problem with the usual result that they danced to some rather carelessly selected classical or modern musical composition. Is this the right method of combining music with the dance? In order to answer this important question, let me take you back to the beginnings of culture and give a brief resumé of the development of these two arts.

It is useless to try to determine whether men first expressed themselves through the medium of gesture or of tone. But as far back as we can see, we know that the dance and music, or movement and tone were performed together. We never find dancing without music, movement without tone. This fact is very significant, for it means that men expressed themselves through two mediums at the same time. It means that man is the bearer of two elements of art which express the same content, the same feelings and emotions. This is, to my mind, the point from which we can proceed to base our conclusions as to the connection between the dance and music. Even today, these two arts are to be found inseparable in the Hindu culture, also appearing together among the Egyptians and many primitive races.

It was not until the Greek culture developed that there was the first sign of separation. This brings us to the next significant point. At the great festivals in ancient Greece, we find for the first time that music was played for its own sake. In this case it was the anlos, a sort of flute that was played. Here also we see the appearance of the musical virtuoso. Thus, the opportunity was presented for music to develop independently of its sister art, the dance.

Music then spread into Western Europe where it held its place, cradled by the Christian church, which demanded the strict separation of music and the dance. The latter was considered an unholy and sinful bodily activity having no connection whatever with church music, which was the only musical form existing at that time. It is interesting to note that the early Christian zealots did not realize that moving before the altar with symbolic gestures was in itself of the nature of the dance. And since this church music was produced by the human voice, it did have a very close relationship to the body. It is important to mention here that music was still only melodic.

But a change of considerable consequence soon came about. Men found that they could sing different tones together, thus developing in European music something that was distinctively different from anything known before. By the singing of several tones together, the element of harmony was brought into music.

With this discovery, the separation of music and the dance became complete. Formerly having been simply a means of human expression, music now became an independent art consisting of the three elements of rhythm, melody and harmony.

No longer was the human voice the only producer of musical expression. Musical instruments were developed bringing with them an independent instrumental music of which the highest form is the sonata or symphony. Here we first encounter the problem of form. In order to trace its development in the symphony, we must go back a step. As I have already said, music had its first place in the church. But with the advent of instrumental music it became separated from the church, in which case it was known as "profane" music. Here it again united with the dance which had found its way into the courts as a form of entertainment. It was at the time that the "profane" music met the "profane" dance that the French and Italian ballets received their original impetus. The Gavottes, Gigues, Pavanes, Minuets and all the numerous dance forms which arose were a product of the life and spirit of the times.

In putting these dance forms together, then, we find that the Suite, which consisted of four movements, was the first instrumental form. Later, significantly, the Suite became the symphony, though in its final form, there was very little trace of its dance origin to be found. From then on, music as an independent art created its own forms and principles to the point where it actually became possible to write down a musical composition. The dance, too, developed its own forms, which are known as those of the ballet, but they were never independent of music. Later the dance was considered to be a sort of step-child of music and therefore not to be taken very seriously.

During this state of affairs, the modern dance appeared. Ballet music proved to be unsatisfactory and the only other form available was the finished classical composition. But as I have already said, this music consisted of definite forms, making it impossible for the dancer to create anything entirely new because he was forced to respect the form of the music. As a result, dance compositions came to be nothing more than interpretations of music. This was not the intention of the latter nor the purpose of the former, so inevitably the results were poor. Consequently, the modern dance went to the other extreme and was performed without any music at all.

Although I am a firm believer in dancing without music, which seems to me to be the only way to find the creative forces of the dance, there is and always will be a trend toward music. For this reason, I believe that there must be a new dance music, a new relationship between the dance and music which will connect the two as a unique form of art.

How is this to be realized? The answer is very brief. It must be done by combining the elements of the two arts. Where this is not possible there can be no connection. Further, having combined the elements, they must be united into one form or still there can be no connection. The elements of an art are nothing more nor less than human expressions, and only when these human expressions are moulded into a form can we speak of art.

Let us recall here what I said in the beginning in regard to music and the dance always being performed together, in order to make clear why I consider this the clue to the solution of our problem. In dancing and singing simultaneously, men expressed nothing but human emotions which have not changed fundamentally throughout the ages.

In the dance these emotions found expression through rhythm and gesture, in music through rhythm and melody. This makes clear the most important points of relation and combination. Both of these arts are based upon rhythm, there being no difference between music and dance rhythm. Both are related to the rhythms found in breathing and other processes of human life. Musical rhythm, however, produces melody, whereas dance rhythm produces gesture, so that in bringing these two together we find their most important relationship.

I have often observed dancers singing while they were creating a dance theme. You will agree that this is an excellent proof of my thesis. The dance melody has to come primarily from the human voice, and ideally, from the dancer's own voice. Very seldom do accompanists have the feeling for the dance so fully developed that they can read the body melody. Thus I believe that it would be good training for the dancer to start his musical education by developing his melodic sense through the medium of his own voice. There is no theory necessary for that, for every normal person can produce simple melodies as easily as he can move. In this manner he acquires a knowledge of the principal musical elements of rhythm and melody as related to the dance.

There are two remaining elements of both arts which must come together. These are harmony in music and space in the dance.

If we consider harmony as being a space-creating musical phenomenon, we seem to have found the relationship of these two elements. But since its foundation is hardly to be found in the primitive nature of man, and as it appears only at the time when the art-form is developing, this idea would be far too materialistic.

As a matter of fact, the actual visible space of a dance movement is something which is absolutely complete in itself. So is a tonal chord, a "musical plastic." Thus space and harmony do not have as much in common as they might appear to have.

When a dancer speaks of space, he does not only, nor even principally mean actual space, but space which signifies something unmaterialistic, unreal, imaginary, which goes beyond the visible outlines of one or more gestures. Out of this feeling springs a need for musical forms which create the same musical space. This is the reason why the modern dancer tends more to the use of chords of non-tonal quality. A simple seventh chord of non-tonal quality has not the mere constructive musical value it would have if seen from the viewpoint of harmony. Because it does not have the architectural consequences of absolute music, it is far more able to create an imaginative feeling of space similar to that produced by the dance gesture. The use of the more dissolved harmonies is of undeniable advantage to a complete integration of the dance and music.

We have now come to the following conclusions: (1) dance rhythm is identical with musical rhythm; (2) dance gesture and melody go together; (3) space and harmony go together.

But there is still form to be discussed. Only when the elements mentioned above grow together, can we speak of art. If we do not find a close relationship between musical form and dance form, then a vital connection will still be impossible. What, then, do we call form in art? Form is the result of an artistic, creative process, a result which is definite and complete and cannot be changed thereafter. Even repetition with other emotional content does not change it.

In music, however, we find quite a different situation than in the dance. As I have already said, classical music had developed some forms which were so final that it was possible to learn them. The fact that there is a great, great difference between the psychology of form in the dance and in music may help to make clear why it is wrong to combine the modern dance with classical music. The reason is that there is an insurmountable discrepancy of form.

Considering music as a vivid human expression, I do not believe that there will be further progress if we use only classical forms. Form in music means the same as form in the dance, both being the result of a creative process. But it seems to me that the modern dance could be a great stimulant to creative musical forces.

40

The actual process of composing dance accompaniments is based entirely upon practical experience and work. It is not possible to give a precise formula for composing dance music as one would outline the form of a sonata or fugue. We must realize that the most direct means of achieving a vital fusion of music and the dance is to create music especially to complement the form of the dance and complete its inner intention.

Each new dance creates its own form. The new dance music should and can be an integral part of this form. In this way the lines of direction for the composition are drawn from the dance itself. The dance music of the future will no longer assert its motive, then proceed on an entirely independent line to develop the direction of already existing musical forms, even those such as the minuet and the gavotte.

The motive or theme of dance music today springs from the actual bodily movement. This is the first principle which the dancer and musician must learn because it is the principle upon which depends the rightness of the composition. From this almost simultaneous birth, the theme grows in unison with the dance to a musical form complete and expressive. Dance music of this kind has the inevitable beauty of necessity and fulfillment which is the criterion of all modern art.

Thus the theory of composition arises from the general approach. We must be aware that there can be different ways of approaching the discovery of the right music for today's dance. I have tried to indicate this in all that I have said above. The greater part remains to be experienced by every one who tries to follow this natural way. A field of experimental work, a virgin soil, is open to every dancer and every musician.

I wish to finish this discussion of dance music by emphasizing the following point. The symphony developed out of the dance forms existing in the seventeenth century. Therefore, might it not be possible that the dance of today should give rise to new musical forms embodying the same emotional content, the same expressions of life, the same elements of form and the same impulse toward the creation of a new art?

PART II
THE MODERN DANCE
IN
AMERICA

L O V E

People painting mansard roofs; people expressing machines and cities in jazz idiom; people with myopia looking at America. . . . New York, North Carolina, Louisiana, New Mexico, Oregon, Kansas. To define a people which lives in as widely varying states as these is at present more than difficult. To define their mode of expression in any art form is an impossibility—that is, if you wish the definition to hold over a period of time. All that can be done is to collect whatever evidence the past offers, arrange it in some sequence, blindly fill in the innumerable lacunae, and then fearfully issue a statement.

That statement must be to a certain extent based on the theory that our first response to a strange environment is undoubtedly physical rather than conceptional; and our first expression of it, whether conscious or unconscious, will be made in physical terms. It is only after this body-adjustment has been made that the mind enters to recount what has been happening. This is where our prognosticators fail. Adrift, utterly unpossessed of the land, they unleash their active minds and think by some mental somersault to possess and express what the body has had no opportunity to learn. It follows, then, that the dance, being a rhythmed expression of our motor impulses and experiences, should be the first art form to cement this reaction to an environment.

The modern American dance is still an infant, even though lusty. Nevertheless, it is beginning to do this: An introductory chapter has been written, but the first chapter, although begun, has not yet come to a period. It will not until the final theories and techniques of at least three contemporary American dancers have been recorded and put into wider practice than they enjoy at the present time. Those three are MARTHA GRAHAM, DORIS HUMPHREY and CHARLES WEIDMAN; their achievements so far will be noted later in this essay.

First we must look backward and the more we look the less there seems to say, in so far as influences are concerned. We find that the first dancing took root in the South, where the English and French court dances were indulged in during the late 17th and early 18th centuries. In the vagabond theatre there were rope dancers, contortionists, harlequinades and hornpipes used between the acts. In 1800 PLACIDE's ballet group and company of tight-rope dancers arrived and exhibited without making any noticeable dent in the American consciousness. In 1827 MME. HUTIN came over from France, bringing with her an inkling of the French ballet as it was at that time. She created somewhat of a stir by showing her legs—or, better, by acknowledging the fact that she had legs. The encasement of subsequent dancers in a more or less complete covering for a time was the result of this indecency. MME. CELESTE and MME. AUGUSTE followed her, the latter in 1836, opening in a scene from the ballet, "Les Naiades." She, according to accounts from that period, was the first important dancer to appear here.

TAGLIONI and ELLSLER followed her in rapid succession. Then when the Academy of Music burned to the ground, a group of European artists was stranded just before its opening. "The Black Crook" was born as a result of the frantic efforts of the manager to make use of them. MARIE BONFANTI, RITA SANGALLI, BETTY RIGL and ROSE DELVAL carried the dancing; the show opened at Niblo's Garden in 1866 and was an instantaneous success. After an amazingly long run, considering the time at which it was produced, it was revived by the KIRALFY family of dancers in 1872. In 1882 they followed it with "Excelsior," with the assistance of SR. ETTORE COPPINI, who later became balletmaster of the Metropolitan Opera Company, and GEORGE SARACCO, who had the main dance role.

These successes gave rise to innumerable imitators which brought a definite period of decline in ballet dancing, until, in the seasons of 1909-10, and 1910-11, the Metropolitan Opera presented the Russian ballet, including such famed dancers as PAVLOWA, LOPOKHOVA, MORDKIN, VOLININE, and GELTZER. Then in 1915-16 and 1916-17, the Diaghileff Ballet presented the newest developments in that particular technique. The result of this influx of ballet was the opening of many schools throughout America. Of the Russian groups, FOKINE and MORDKIN, among others, later came here to teach.

Two forms of ballet have been stronger than any others in influencing the American attitude toward dancing. The first was the academic classical ballet developed in France; the second, the more romantic method that matured in Russia through ISADORA DUNCAN's recitals in St. Petersburg in the early 1900's. But the influence, it must be noted, was upon the spectator, not upon the dancer. The ballet still remains dominant in vaudeville and the theatre but, despite this contact, no American dancer worthy of the name has been identified with this technique and there has been nothing what we could call an American ballet in the technical sense of the word.

Meanwhile, there were occasional rumblings throughout America, scarcely heard at that time but now, in the light of developments within the past ten or fifteen years, taking on a much larger importance. The Indians, on their reservations, continued their ceremonial rituals, and the Negroes, in the outlands, laid the foundations of jazz. But neither of these in the beginning of things, had any important influence.

During an earlier period, the Can-Can came over from Montmarte dance

47

halls and created the American high-kicker. AMELIA BLOOMER has already assured herself of a place in the dictionary by freeing the ladies from their usual reticent encasements. LOTTIE COLLINS preluded jazz with contortion and frenzied action added to the high-kicking. Meanwhile LOIE FULLER was shifting from Temperance lectures to dancing, and from that to voice culture, which settled her temporarily as an "actress with a singing part." It was during one of these engagements that the inspiration came to her in the form of a gift from India, a silk scarf, whose possible undulations gave birth to the multicolored Serpentine Dance. Almost overnight she became famous in New York and later in Paris, thrilling audiences with the movement of drapery.

For further freeing the local inhibitions, there were JACK BROUGHTON, the inventor of the boxing glove; FRIEDRICH FROEBEL, who began the kindergarten; EMILE JACQUES-DALCROZE, who developed a theory of dance in relation to music, and IRENE and VERNON CASTLE, innovators in ballroom dancing.

In 1893 the World's Fair in Chicago introduced America to the Oriental dance. This naive exposure brought a storm of swooning disgust and the charge of low obscenity. The managers smiled and agreed and forced their dancers to accentuate whatever might accord with this definition. Accordingly, America saw little of the Oriental dance as a complete form and added one more tabu to cuticle-exposure which is still existent at this moment.

And now, having cursorily inventoried the 19th century, we have not touched upon anything that could be called the American dance. Only one fact dominates this clutter, and that is that America was, in trite terms, ready for a revolution.

ISADORA DUNCAN made her first preliminary gesture in a little theatre in Chicago in 1899. DELSARTE's natural-pantomime had come in a perverted form to America and influenced her. She had made a brief beginning in ballet technique, which was still the only respectable professional method that was taught here, and gave it up. She had come in contact with Greek art, with the result that loose-flowing gowns, bare feet and "movement from nature" became the only important things for her. She insisted on the slightly draped human body, plus bare feet and limbs, which was, of course, a shock to her spectators for some time.

It was her Russian recitals that participated the vague rumblings that had already been heard in the Imperial Ballet and caused it to change from French to Russian. These results America saw when the Diaghileff Ballet arrived in 1915.

The period of her own personal theoretical influence was brief. No dancers who followed her surpassed or even equalled her; rather they were lost in the vague emotionalism her work invoked. Nevertheless, whether or not she herself evolved them, many of her written notes are basic today and constitute a clear background structure for the modern dance. Rhythm was no longer synonymous with beat but came to mean a sequence of self-evolved movements, harmonized with the fundamental pulse and flow of the body-rhythms and capable of repetition. The term "movement" was changed. According to accepted definition, it was synonymous with motion and meant a change of weight or position. Now motion came to mean a change of weight without particular purpose (the mere physical fact of ceasing to be static), whereas movement took to itself a distinct connotation of purpose, because movements were used only in relation to a central dynamo or motor power, which ISADORA located in the chest, the seat of the two vital rhythms of the body, blood and breath. The shift in the meaning of dance was one from line to mass, from building by accretion to organic evolution. ISADORA's imitators, and ISADORA

49

herself, carried all this too far into the lily-zephyr trend; yet it remains.

As ISADORA was beginning her activities, RUTH ST. DENIS had a vision of the dance. While acting under the management of DAVID BELASCO, she saw a cigarette poster of an Egyptian goddess, which apparently converged with her previous ideas and hopes. It was not long before she was creating a series of East Indian ballets, which were followed by more important incursions into Egyptian and Far Eastern Oriental forms. A clever theatrical sense carried these pantomime-dances over at first; later they were deepened by an intensive study of Oriental methods. The attempt at musical-visualization, which was started in the Denishawn School, grew directly from her having seen ISADORA and having noted her use of music as a substructure for movement.

ISADORA DUNCAN and RUTH ST. DENIS, then, are the only two originators we possess. ISADORA's contributions were: 1: a reversal to forgotten dance forms (in her case Greek) so as to relate the dance once more to life and to make it an art-expression rather than mere entertainment; 2: a theory of movement based on natural flow, without the ballet starts and stops; 3: a significant death-blow to the traditional ballet technique. Her major deficiency was the use of inspiration as an impetus, which meant that no workable form was created. In technique she advanced postures taken from Greek sculpture and vases, some of the ballet code, and a great deal of pantomime, without achieving a fusion that might be carried on by other dancers.

RUTH ST. DENIS' contributions were: 1: gestures and movements taken from the Orient, from Egypt, and from the American Indian; 2: a clearer knowledge of theatrical presentation; 3: musica-visualization, in an attempt to reach some form. Unfortunately, neither of these formal experiments achieved any tangible results, ISADORA's depending on the subjective, introvertive approach to music, and St. Denis' depending on the close imitation of musical pattern to such an extent that each dancer became no more than a replica of some instrument in the orchestra work presented.

In this brief summary of the dance in America, the record has now been brought up to the War. One feels quite sure that somehow the American dance has begun but that it is quite undefinable. It was the sudden evolution of a German technique that struck America next. Inklings arrived through the press. In a short time this new development was being exhibited sporadically by students of Laban and Wigman.

In trying to locate influences, we are striking uncertain ground. In the late 1920's there was a sudden flowering of American dancers, of which the three surest and most completely developed were Martha Graham, Doris Humphrey and Charles Weidman. We may attribute in a large degree their impetus to the dance from Isadora and from the Denishawns, and their clarification of purpose in some degree to the new-born German dance. Yet they themselves contributed a new revolt and the theories which began to take form at this time had been incubating before the German dance evolved. They were working toward abstraction, toward classicism, toward a consciousness of America, and the influences from the three sources mentioned were only incidental. They were original, creative dancers, all three of them trying to place the dance on an architectural basis.

The ballet technique for them was meaningless and artificial. Romantic self-expression was tabu. Narratives and literary sketches executed in movement were no longer their concern. Each one of them realized that the dance must have form, must be built with the solidity and functionalism of architecture, must express something that only movement in an ordered rhythm could express.

G R A H A M

To THE AMERICAN DANCER I SAY: "Know our country." When its vitality, its freshness, its exuberance, its overabundant youth and vigor, its contrasts of plentitude and barrenness are made manifest in movement on the stage, we begin to see the American dance.

Nothing is more revealing than movement. What you are finds expression in what you do. The dance reveals the spirit of the country in which it takes root. No sooner does it fail to do this than the dance begins to lose its indispensable integrity and significance.

Take as example a group of young American dancers in an Oriental dance. What they do they do well. But we are looking upon theatrics. Nothing more. An impression of Oriental dancing which consisted mainly of an effective decoration on the stage is attempted. This alone is achieved. The decoration is enjoyed; the impression is unforgettable. It has nothing however to do with the dance of America.

America does not concern itself now with impressionism. We own no involved philosophy. The psyche of the land is to be found in its movement. It is to be felt as a dramatic force of energy and vitality. We move; we do not stand still. We have not yet arrived at the stock-taking stage.

As we begin to take more and more honor in the interpretation of the American scene, our dance takes deeper and deeper root.

The traditions of one country are not those of another. When we speak of America, it is of an accumulation of forces inherent only to this soil. As certain metals are tempered in specific temperatures, so is the individual tempered in the land he lives. In the dancer is to be mirrored the tempo and essential rhythm of his country.

To attempt to free oneself of this heritage means escape that bears no fruit. It has been common practice to seek instruction in lands alien to us, fettered as we are to things European. What does this mean? It means to me losing all that we should hold most dear in the development of the American dance.

We do not speak of the rise of a cult, jingoistic and shortsighted, hewing to the narrow limits of nationalism. We share, but we share with others what is ours, not theirs. The flavor of America is in and of this country; the results are transmitted to all countries to see. The dancer finds his material here; he dances where he wishes.

The dance has been peculiarly the sufferer in this country of this unwillingness to dig deep into our own experience. The escape motif which has so long blinded the artistic vision of the American artist has made of our dancers too often imitators of a culture utterly foreign to us. We cannot transplant the foreign dance-forms, and we fight in a vain effort to breathe life into them. Enthusiasm is no apology for misdirection.

America must develop its own dance. It means first an intensive training period for the dancer here. We are gradually winning public acceptance to years of preparatory training in the development of a dancer, although it has by no means been fully achieved yet. For the hopeful mother still brings her five year old child to the studio with a plea to have her child ready for exhibition dancing in three months.

Nor have we yet entirely succeeded in ridding men of the grotesque notion that the art of the dance is essentially effeminate. Here nothing could be further from the truth. The heritage of the Indian dance, with its intense integration, our activity, the power and sweep of our perpendicular architecture—these do not speak of things effeminate.

A dancer trains vigorously. He does an amazing amount of hard work. Learning how to dance is not a parlor game. A training period teaches people how to dance, reveals the rudiments of the dance, gives them the necessary suppleness of the body, the proper perspective.

A dance technique may be learned wherever there are expert dance teachers. But the tendency to leave one's country during the tremendously important formative years means making an unnecessary sacrifice. It means leaving the current of one's country. It means leaving a characteristic rhythm of which we must be part in forming the dance of our own country.

Technique is but one integral element necessary to the formation of a dancer.

The American dancer may, but need not, go abroad to acquire a dance technique. He must not go to acquire an alien manner and form.

The modern American dance began here. Here it must stay and flourish. Isadora Duncan, the greatest individual stimulus to the dance of modern times, looked to America to develop her dance. Only when the art of her dance had been fully formed did she turn to Europe to have them share her genius with her. The spirit of her dance: its rhythm, vitality, new freedom of the body, the modern influences—all these were of America.

When we speak of this country, we speak of a vast concept, whose infinite facets cannot all be seen. But in this immensity let us find the fundamentals of which we are all part.

Let us examine for a moment a striking difference in the continent's and our own reaction to an important factor of modern times—the machine.

Talk to the continental, talk to the American of the machine's part in the tempo of modern life. The reactions are unmistakably characteristic.

To the European the machine is still a matter of wonder and excessive sentimentality. Some sort of machine dance is a staple to every European dance repertory. But to the American sentimentality for the machine is alien. The machine is a natural phenomenon of life. Make use of it. Suit it to our needs. Integrate it into our activities. But the machine as an object of veneration in and of itself, that is simply non-American. No American dance I know represents the machine. The dancer of America does not glorify mechanized movement, which so completely concerned the ballet. He no longer considers protests against the mechanization of life. He sees the machine as one of the many products of human skill, and then considers its work.

This is simply one of the fundamental characteristics of our country.

We have seen in the intensive preparations of long years a way to technique, of movement based upon the body as a positive instrument functioning in certain ways. But what of the rest of the dancer's art?

An American dance is not a series of new steps. It is more, infinitely more. It is a characteristic time beat, a different speed, an accent, sharp, clear, staccato. We know the American expression; we see the American gesture. Of things American the American dance must be made.

It demands that we shun the pallid hot-house sentimentalities of interpretive dancing, the traditional ballet, the involved philosophy of the Orient. We do not consider now, nor deny, the value of these forms in and of themselves, nor the good they have wrought to a dance history. But they are not of us. What they have sought to express, we no longer create. We deny their influence over us, and embark upon our own art-form.

To do otherwise would mean an art without substance, without integrity, with no meaning.

To seek then the essential spirit of the country, to impart its sense of life, to enrich, illuminate, and intensify the American scene becomes then the object of the American dancer.

To whom, other than himself, may he turn for his material?

Our task is to create a subject matter, significant and contemporary, for the American dancer. Until now, it has largely been the task of the dancer himself. This is not so in music, generally, nor on the dramatic stage. The interpreter then is rarely the creator.

But the dancer faces also the duties of a choreographer. Sometimes the union is a perfect one. Sometimes it is not. I see no reason why a great dancer need necessarily be a great choreographer. Why shall we not be able to turn for subject matter to an American choreographer in whose material the dancer shall have something significant to dance, of his own time, of his own understanding.

The choreographer has great deeds to perform. It is he, technically trained as a dancer, who will create a dance-form in manner and style typically American. He will look to no other country for guidance in creative work, for he is a man born of America, and in his outlook will be one with his country. He will supply a dance-form sympathetic and understandable to the American point of view.

The task is great. It requires the choreographer to be trained as a dancer. It requires that he sensitize himself to his country, that he know something of its history, its political and geographic life. He will see something of the inside of his country, leaving the cosmopolitan seaport. He will know the people of the coast of New England, the spirit of the West, the rugged grandeur of the

Rockies. He will have a drive which will enable him to direct and correlate these experiences into significant compositions of movement.

As we increasingly have something significant to dance, we shall find more and more persons to dance for.

No great dance can leave a people unmoved. Sometimes the reaction will take the form of a cold antagonism to the truth of what they are seeing. Sometimes an unbelievable response. What is necessary is that the dance be as strong as life itself, and of the life that is known in the country, that it be influenced by the prevailing expression of the people of a country, as well as by the geography of the land itself.

But to the audience of America the American dance owes a duty. It cannot lull them into complacency by presenting a decorative or imitative dance-form as the product of this country. The dance is no easy solution to light entertainment. The American dance is not an effeminate art-form. This wrong conditioning has gone on too long. We look to America to bring forth an art as powerful as this country. We look to the dance to impart the sensation of living in an affirmation of life, to energize the spectator into keener awareness of the vigor, the mystery, the humor, the variety, and the wonder of life. This is the function of the American dance.

H U M P H R E Y

Through the only serious and intensive training which was available in America at the time, the Denishawn method, DORIS HUMPHREY learned in great detail the Oriental dance and the sentamentalized classicism set up by ISADORA. She knew the ballet technique. She had been experimenting with the group dance and with the interaction of music and the dance. It was from this jumbled background that her present theory was developed, more in coincidence with this training than because of it. It grew from her acquired knowledge plus a strong rhythmic sense and, in addition to these and overlaying them, her personal reactions to what was called modern American life.

Elements of her stature which were in evidence before the Denishawn break have remained and deepened. The first was a supple versatility of body, coupled with an intelligence that was beginning to attain a complete consciousness of the difference between a strong and a weak lyricism; between a pointless posturing and essential movement; between a tableau arrangement and the deeper inner organization of the group. Other influences were an undeveloped but certain trend away from solo and toward the group choreography, and an intimacy with musical structure and feeling. These are closely interrelated and interactionary and may be summed up as a personal awareness of Form and a personal ability to create it. This feeling for Form as a necessity had been vaguely stated by the romantic movement, but the romanticism that colored their so-called classical theories was powerful enough to prevent their reaching any conclusions, except the dependence on musical structure as support.

Miss Humphrey's sense of the body as an organism and her adaptability to choreographic structure caused her for a while to dispense with music almost entirely, until she came to a closer apprehension of kinesthetic as distinguished from musical rhythm and built units established on the body flow rather than on the musical beat. Because of the reactions that inevitably followed from this body sense, she turned more deeply into herself and realized the possible stultification of her own movement, if it were allowed to remain too long in the curve. The change was stated finally in the solo dance, "Ecstatic Themes," which was divided into a Circular Descent and a Pointed Ascent. The counterpoint of sharp and soft, of angular and circular, while still lyrical, was now far stronger than before. The conclusions of her research and her slow but concise probing were stated technically in the group dance, "Pleasures of Counterpoint", and brilliantly (in relation to subject matter) in the "Dionysiaques" that followed.

The purpose of Miss Humphrey's experimentation has been to arrive at a useable and understandable definition of rhythm. The process of creation that was based almost entirely on emotion, on inspiration, was too likely to reach its purposed conclusion by chance, and that chance was too sporadic. This means that a firm technical basis must be arrived at before she would be able to become as organically concise in form as she might have been previously in idea or in isolated sequences. And the only final approach to this is through the head. A dance may be conceived emotionally but it must be built intellectually. In the last analysis, then, the approach was only partially to a definition of rhythm. Actually, it was an attempt to isolate, to analyze, to dissect, and then to reorganize the Substance of the dance, which, in its two main phases in America so far, had leaned in one toward a cold mechanical technicalism in the ballet and in the other toward a diffuse, vague improvisation in the romantic school.

Motion is generated by force. Where a force acts upon the body without opposition or resistance, the motion is into infinity. Where two equal and opposing forces act upon a body, that body remains motionless. Where there is a force inherent in a body, which balances and neutralizes forces, there is form or mass. In the motional phenomena of inorganics, there is only a smooth and monotonous flow whose perpetual continuity in one unchanged degree of tension robs it of our usual intellectual conception of movement.

This motion is one phase of the movement of organic matter. For example, we might note the response of our own skeletal structure to stimuli, the necessity of moving. In contrast to this, there are certain Hindu fakirs who sit motionless for years. They are introducing a new element: the human mind, which is a conscious force that is attempting to equalize the unconscious, natural forces.

The first thing that differentiates it is the consciousness of the object who produces it. It may be called the Creative Force, the Creative Impulse, the Will to Move, as distinguished from the other which is Natural Existence, Organic Inertia. It is certainly cumulative, certainly combative. In varying degree it exists in all organic forms and is primarily composed of two elements: the one, Resistance; the other, Creation. It is a movement that attempts, that builds, that creates, that analyzes and recombines its materials. In addition to this, it is a movement that is in continual resistance against the other motion that works toward balance, toward inertia. The only dynamism of life, then, is the product of these two: the interaction of the unconscious and the conscious, the unconditioned and the conditioned, the Natural Existence and the Creative Force.

Having come so far, we are close to the general theories of modern science, to the explanation of modern life, to the prominence of jazz. There is nothing fixed. We have become aware of two poles, both of which are death. The death of motionlessness (stasis) lies on the one side; the death of destruction (loss of balance) lies on the other.

Miss Humphrey has called movement the arc between two deaths. Thus, movement is essentially unbalance, and the degree of unbalance conditions the intensity of the movement. That is, the amount of distortion of a movement determines its tension. Rhythm is the result of the organization of these parts (these tension-stages) into a unified whole.

There is no Being (which would be a permanent stoppage at either of the poles) but only a continual Becoming between these two poles of immobility. Thus, the basis of the dance, as of all art, is Conflict. The conflict between the will to calm and the will to danger engenders movement. The conflict of a traditional gesture and a dance gesture engenders emotion. The conflict of one direction with another direction engenders Form. The conflicts of line-direction create pattern or linear design; the conflicts of mass-direction create volume or spatial design, etc.

Her conclusions are really the intersection between the ballet and the romantic methods that were dominant when she began to dance. It should be immediately discernible that the ballet has leaned in excess toward the Creative Impulse, which explains the deadened mathematical technicalism that has resulted; that the romantic movement has leaned in excess toward the Natural Existence, which explains the vagueness and formlessness it has reached. An excess in one direction leads to Diagram; in the other to Formlessness. Form can only result from a careful inter-balance of these two.

The whole study of the dance for Miss Humphrey may be divided into Natural Technique, Distorted Technique, Composition, and Projection. It is necessary to analyze the subject matter to be presented; describe the choice of all possible natural movements; make selections from these; and point them by styling, distorting or exaggerating. The movement, since it is to be contained in the box stage, must be projected in only one direction. Every vital movement, every change, every opposition must be entirely visible from a single point.

In actual teaching, she divides movement into three phases: Rhythm, Design (in Time and in Space) and Dynamics, each of which concentrates on one particular aspect of movement. Viewed as a whole, each exercise contains the complete elements; it is only the emphasis on one part that differentiates it from another.

The Rhythm exercises specify the duality (the conflict) which is the basis of rhythmic movement: fall and recovery, which visualizes the two poles, at each of which the motion might cease. In a sense, this is little more than natural movement emphasized for clarity. The purpose is not the teaching of a rhythm to be learned and used later. It is to arouse a body-feeling and make body adjustments in the student. Thus, the initial emphasis is on feeling, on the definitely receptive reaction of the body to the particular movement. When the body is not repeating it mechanically by rote, but has accepted it and has complete control of it, then the "count" is analyzed and learned; and following this, accent. To make a bridge between the two, the accent may be placed at first in a simple routine order, coinciding with the strongest body movement. Later it shifted to the weaker movement, preceding or following the strong movement. By becoming an off-accent, it increases the student's feeling of the body and also increases the strength of the strong movement, which has to depend on itself alone for accent.

In the Design exercises, there is emphasis on the spatial and the temporal aspects. Design in Space is a movement seen only as an accent. Thus, a leap in the air is a design in space. It is the pattern of the figure in the air and not the few seconds of leaving the ground and returning to it which are remembered. The Design of Time has reference to the movement which takes some time to be completed. For a simple example, we might take the body that is moving in a straight line, while the arm is slowly rising and completing an arc over the head. It will take several footsteps before the arm has finished its pattern.

Under the Design exercises, there are four "headings;" Opposition, Succession, Unison and Distortion. They are, again, isolated for emphasis, but are applicable to any sort of exercises. The Rhythm exercises were chiefly related to the natural movement, but here, where there is more obvious working toward composition, the emphasis is on distorted or stylized movement. (Distortion, it will be clearly understood, is not a "funny-looking" peculiar move-ment. It means no more than a change from the natural and is referable to Greek sculpture as well as to the most extreme modernistic dance.) The emphasis on Succession is on flow, on overlapping movement, which may move from one in-dividual to another, from one movement to another, or from one group-segment to another. New movements arise before the preceding ones have reached their termination; new directions are taken before the old direction dies; new rhythms begin in the reverberations of the rhythms before. It is, to a large extent, the suc-cession which gives the dance form. (A succession may, likewise, be occasionally stopped on an accent, in which case it becomes a design in space. If the flow has been well stated before the accent-step is made, it may continue again without loss of connection, provided, of course, that the interval of cessation is not long. This is the same thing that holds true in music, where too great an interval makes the following rhythm unable to establish its connection.)

Unison refers to the perfectly balanced symmetrical positions that may be used for one body or for the group. Opposition may refer to the natural alternation of arms and legs during walking, or it may be distorted, for example, in the arm patterns during a walking movement. When the legs are apart, in their stride, the arms form an X-cross over the chest, the hands pointing vertically upward. Then, as the legs come together in the next step, the arms are extended horizontally, the hands facing the body and vertical as before. With the next step they are drawn in again, etc.

In Dynamics, the emphasis is entirely on the degrees of tension, starting with the greatest tension plus the greatest relaxation and working through the innumerable variations of this. In other words, tension becomes synonymous with tempo. Normal tempo corresponds to our breathing, walking, etc. Quickening or slowing the movement gives it color. This is again distortion, a change from the natural.

At this point, it might be remarked that this entire theory is nothing more than the tension-relaxation theory presented by the Germans several years ago. But, although the terms tension and relaxation are still in use, it will be noted that the prominent words are balance and unbalance, and between the two groups there is a distinct difference. The German theory works almost completely on a physical-muscular basis; thus, tension becomes strain and indicates a peak of muscular energy; and relaxation, simply through physical limitations, becomes a degree of exhaustion. Balance and unbalance are the shifting between the poles of immobility; there may be strain and exhaustion, or there may not be. The chief aim is a perpetual balancing between the poles, whereas the Germans are more inclined to carry their efforts to an extreme. They approach the destruction-pole too closely and stay near it too continuously, so that their only possibility finally is to return to the stasis-pole for a longer interval than should be necessary, or to arrive at the destruction pole, which means to fall on the floor.

To clarify MISS HUMPHREY's theories in more visual terms, it might be well to dissect a single rhythm from one of her group dances. The 9-8 rhythm from "The Shakers" is pertinent.

The dance simply represents the Shaker sect at meeting and is a study of religious ecstacy. It opens with the dancers kneeling in a square formation before the platform where the elders sit. A religious frenzy seizes them, the square begins to break; the men and the women form two distinct groups, advancing and retreating. Finally, as the frenzy abates, one by one they freeze into an attitude of tense waiting, until the whole group is motionless. Previous to the phrase under consideration, the two groups have been advancing and retreating with monotonous hopping movements, always stopping short at an invisible center line. The new rhythm is begun by a single dancer in the men's group and gradually imparts itself to the others. It takes the form of a falling run forward, coming to an abrupt stop at the center; a push diagonally forward on the floor, accompanied by a down-thrust of the arms; a push diagonally back with the same foot; a swinging turn toward the audience on the standing foot; and a falling run back over the same path to the starting point, with a swift turn at the finish to leave the body in the same position in which the whole phrase began.

The approach to the dance was through natural movement. The run was used by the Shakers, but might contain few or many steps; it was bound to stop at an imagined division line, because the males and females were separated into groups; it might take some time to impart it to the whole group, after it had been begun by one member. Compositionally, then, the run must be limited to a set pace, for three important reasons: because of its natural origin, because of the stage on which it would be set, and because of the necessity of form. It must explain the original emotion and, at the same time, maintain the group in a tightly organized unit. The communication of the rhythm gradually to the entire group must be ordered so as to appear spontaneous and yet avoid the helter-skelter of the actual meeting. This means that its repetition must be in a distinct ratio, so that it can be rapid and likewise illustrate the emotion it conveys to the participants. It must create for the audience a clear sense of the division line It must contain design in time to give continuity, design in space for accent.

First, we must take account of the physical limitation of the center line, for that very largely determined the basic form. The run started on the right side of the stage, and five steps (beginning on the left foot) brought the body almost to the line. The impetus was such that the body was off-balance, so the right foot was pushed against the floor in front to check the motion and give it new direction backwards. To prevent falling in this opposite direction, the same foot was pushed against the floor in back, thus catching the weight of the body and once more throwing it forward. Unless this process were repeated indefinitely, which it might very well have been, there was no alternative except a turn. So the pushing of the right foot backwards was accompanied by a falling turn around the stationary left foot as pivot, the right leg describing a complete arc in the air and effecting an about-face of the body. The momentum of this swing prevented any immediate stopping and had to lose itself in a long run along the same path back to the starting point. By the time it had reached this point, equilibrium was regained so that the body could gather itself for a quick turn.

Here, then, was the skeletal form, the design, with which the rhythm and intensity are inextricably bound. The difference in Time-value between the running steps, the pushes and the swing provide the staccato, regular beat, which emphasized the required emotion and was in contrast with the more regular beat of the preceding sections.

The emotion was already contained in the form, but it was further intensified by slightly dragging the feet on the runs, thus increasing the sensation of falling; by freeing the body from any stiffening or controlling force during the swing; and by extending the falling run backwards beyond the time when the body might have been assumed to have caught its balance.

It is in the process of accent and intensification that the arms play their most important part. At the beginning, they were folded at the elbow so that the back of the clenched fist lay against the shoulder joint. During the run they were slowly lowered and straightened preparatory to thrusting sharply forward and down at the center line, thus accenting the pushing foot. They hung loose during the swing, again to increase the sensation of falling, and likewise during the run back, with the body stooping somewhat. At the end they were returned to the initial position to mark the completion of the phrase and to be in readiness for its repetition.

Thus, they served to clarify the larger movements of the phrase; the tension of the beginning; the seeming unbalance of the middle; and the return to tension at the end, which was likewise the new beginning.

We see that form and content react upon one another and emerge as a unit, simultaneously and inseparably. This gives an air of rightness to the movement, which could not be achieved by a more arbitrary method of squeezing content into form or vice versa. Each movement contains the death of the preceding one and the birth of the following, as well as its own peculiar nature. It is the phrase rather than the individual movement that is the integer. No one of the movements in the 9-8 rhythm could be separated from the whole without affecting all the others and causing a new distribution of the parts. The whole phrase is a conflict between fall and recovery, between balance and unbalance.

And, having come so far through a theory of movement, its possibilities and combinations, there is only one more note to be added. That refers to the content of the dance. Miss HUMPHREYS says, "In choosing a theme for a dance, theoretically I claim the world, at least the Western World, as possible material. By this I mean to include the arts, the industries, the legendry, history, and the sciences, even to biology and psychology, of modern and ancient times. Also I have my own interior world of sensation to work with, and the meaning of my experience. Personally, I think the dancer is safest in sticking to this latter theme to insure artistic integrity. This is a very different outlook for the dancer from that presented even ten years ago. Then and before, the ballet was in the foreground with stories exclusively fairy-like or romantic. ISADORA DUNCAN and RUTH ST. DENIS came and widened the horizon, but still kept well within the romantic scope. A machine dance was unheard of. Then the dance reached out with the rest of the aesthetic world and now seems able to delve into almost every crack and corner of it. Almost, but not quite. For me, at least, I have come to recognize certain ground that is tabu. Hence I said that the world is ours theoretically. Practically, it is not. In the first place, some themes, however stirring to the imagination they may be, are static in their essence and do not permit of a movement treatment. Now movement is the very bones and blood of the modern dance and must first, last and always be dominant in it. For this reason static ideas are dangerous. They tend to stop the flow of movement."

In striking the theory of balance and unbalance, Miss Humphrey has struck close to modern psychology. Her themes, and those of many modern dancers, are far from the passive loveliness of the previous era. They infer danger, excitement, struggle, intellectual probing. "For people in other times and countries, a common religion had been so well-established, at least during the life-span of any one artist, that he was provided with a ready-made attitude toward experience. He knew what the past meant, what he could expect from the future, and therefore with what it was important to concern himself in the present. But the modern artist is adrift in a maelstrom of conflicting interpretations of life and must determine truths for himself by an individual analysis." If he is able to develop a theory which, in its very technique, is able to concretize the conflict of modern life, he has reached, for him, a stability, a balance; and it is that inner balance which is essential before an art-form can come into being . . . . an art form, that is, which will have more than momentary existence.

W E I D M A N

It must not be forgotten that, up to the early 1900's, the dance had been so busy with geometry and so far from contact with the still-existing forms, that it had almost lost any sense of the body as a natural organism. Decades rolled by before even such innocent members as legs were allowed public exhibition without some sort of covering, and, by the time they were more or less accepted, the code of movement had become so rigid that a small revolution was needed in order to break it.

Since there was no tight and communicable technique built up from this return to natural movement, it is difficult to state concisely what the term meant at that time. It was used chiefly to express, or attempt to express, the more serious themes that the dancers were developing. Since they were too much involved with the "soul" and with idealized beauty, it was not at the beginning a basis of physical study for the dancer, but rather a means of conveying vague emotions which the rigid ballet could not convey.

It was while this so-called new sense of movement was being felt out, wondered at and experimented with, that CHARLES WEIDMAN was receiving his initial instruction at the Denishawn School. The dance was still more or less of a feminine proceeding, but he possessed two important qualities that carried him across and negated whatever of the decadent male technique he may have been taught. The one was an inherent pantomimic sense, which verged closer to comedy than tragedy. The other was a developing consciousness of the meaning of Form, which gave the pantomimic sense power and caused him to be dissatisfied with the trite current gestures and attitudes.

71

He was impelled toward a movement method that would be strong and vigorous and masculine; that would have natural physical movement as its substructure but would not confine itself to this limited circle in the dance forms he might create.

His break with the Denishawn School in the 1920's and his relationship with DORIS HUMPHREY clarified many of the difficulties. He had his own groups of men to work with, but he was also in close contact with the similar theoretical training that was being done by MISS HUMPHREY. This interaction between the two gave him a clearer general view of movement in relation to men and to women than he might have achieved had he been working entirely with men. Thus he was able to obtain a more complete realization of the natural movement-modes common to both sexes, and the variations that distinguish one from the other.

The physical structure of a man's body must be taken into account in all its ramifications, for it is the variations, the degrees of muscular strength and muscular reaction alone that will make the true distinction. This does not mean that he was forced to evolve particular movements and rhythms that are never used by women, but rather that he must know the quantity of certain ones in proportion to others, and the quality of any one that might be used by both men and women.

This may be clearer if we think for a moment of a specific movement. Suppose the dancer's body, with feet stable and separated, leans diagonally forward and raises the arms upward and forward from their natural hanging position to a horizontal position. For expression this might be used by either sex in the evolution of a particular dance. In the first place, WEIDMAN would dissect the movement carefully for its content possibilities; in the second place, he would note the variations of quality, in regard to its masculine and its feminine side and in regard to its meaning.

In the rigid categories that even now, to a certain extent, surround the dance, this movement might very well be given a precise definition, and it would enter the vocabulary of the dancer in one specifically qualified, unmoveable form. In other words, it would no more be subject to variation in form than would one of the letters of the alphabet. This is based on the assumption that every movement has a particular meaning, which is a falsehood. Recalling the illustration mentioned briefly above, you will realize that it may mean almost any number of things, *depending on the intensity behind it*. It may be aggressiveness, resignation, sorrow, disgust, yearning, etc. Accordingly, WEIDMAN states that intensification denotes the meaning; that a movement by itself (that is, in its generalized form) contains no meaning whatsoever. This theory connotes a continuous consciousness of the differentiation between the feminine and masculine reaction under identical circumstances, and between the reaction of one individual and that of another.

In training his dancers, WEIDMAN begins with the natural laws of movement and insists upon the repetition of them until the body is felt surely as an entity governed by these laws. After the laws are realized, the execution becomes personal and even the least developed person will be different in his presentation from every one else. In actual method, this realization of the individuality of the dancer is to a certain extent a neat balance between the romantic method begun by ISADORA DUNCAN and the set, controlled curriculum of the ballet. The latter made a differentiation between the tall and the short dancer, and between the bow-legged and the knock-kneed one, but as a general rule, this allowed only the cutting off of a few isolated movements from each dancer's technique. In method he was forced to achieve certain definite results and was rarely allowed to alter the movements according to personal idiosyncrasies. In the DUNCAN method, there was no catalog whatever; there was only the soul of the dancer which told him when and how to move, and, unfortunately enough, even this soul was usually not his own but was superimposed by the inspired teacher.

WEIDMAN's method is based on a few primary movement-phrases, whose purpose in the beginning is to reveal the dancer's body to him. They are abstract, as the ballet steps are, but they are not superimposed upon the dancer and they are not exercises on isolated parts of the body unrelated to other parts and to the body as a whole. They are natural in the sense that they are not in the least feats or skill which have to be plugged at for a long period of time before they can be learned. Being natural, they can be easily adapted to his specific powers by each dancer who learns them. Each exercise is a series of movements with beginning and end and with form so that, in a sense, it is a small dance or a small rhythm that may be incorporated into a dance. The student thus learns not only his physical potentialities but also a sequence or succession which at the very beginning reveals the possibilities of developing a movement into other movements and other rhythms. Composition, in short, is not something that is tacked on after the alphabet is learned.

There is a simple pushing-up exercise which it might be worth examining at this point. The dancer lies face downward on the floor with the arms against the sides. As the drum beat begins, he turns over, crossing the left leg over the right and drawing the foot close to the pelvic region to make one support for the following movement. Naturally, in the turn, the torso is raised so that the body makes an oblique angle on the floor. The right arm supports the raised torso (natural opposition) and the left is flexed bringing the clenched fist against the pelvic region. This is really preparation for the major movement that follows. As the pelvis is raised from the floor to bring the body into a slightly arched tension (still supported by the right arm and the left leg) the flexed arm is simultaneously raised and straightened over the head. Then the body is slowly lowered again, turned, and returned to its initial position.

Although the stress may be laid at first entirely on physical development, it is later used to illustrate natural opposition and natural succession. By the natural law of succession, WEIDMAN means the unfolding of one part after another from a center. In this case, the pelvic region is the center, although it may not always be. The raising of the body into a tension comes through this region, and its source is accentuated by the flexed arm, whose movement grows upward likewise (visually, at least) out of this center.

Variations in tempo, in accent, in quality may easily be applied to this natural movement in order to give it different strength and meaning. It is in this process that a consciousness of distortion enters, and WEIDMAN says, "The more one distorts, the better the dance. You have seen natural movement moving from a center in logical succession. These centers or sources of succession may be and are located in different parts of the body. Now, instead of moving these parts naturally, they are moved in a more unusual and unexpected manner. The result will hinge on a personal characteristic . . . one's own ability to organize and relate them properly."

Distortion is simply a changing from the natural shape. It is used in the dance chiefly to describe those changes which are closer to the extreme than they are to the norm. WEIDMAN uses it in several ways: as a series of accents in a particular movement, where the transitions are deleted; as a series of almost unrelated accents in succession; as the deletion of the oppositional preparation for a movement.

In the first case, he might use as a basis an oppositional movement through the body, where the leg is raised from the floor to the side, the opposite arm is extended horizontally for balance, and the head is turned to the side in opposition to the arm. This is a movement in space and takes place simultaneously in all the members. For distortion and accent, the movement is separated into its three parts; the leg is raised; then the arm; then the head; in quick succession so that it becomes a movement in time as well. In a sense, it takes three distinct movements to attain the same end that could be reached in one flowing movement. Nevertheless, it is a single one because of the successional order of the parts, so that the spectator's eye is forced to traverse the three "spots" before he comes to the conclusion.

In the second case, which is far the most difficult, he relies largely on the succession in time to hold the unrelated parts together and give them unity. Usually, if this is to maintain the continuity and not cause a break, it must be preceded by a well-established rhythmic continuity.

The third case, (deletion of the preparation) is very similar to the second, but may be applied to a single movement instead of to a phrase. For example, a leap in the air to the right is naturally preceded by a swing out to the left in preparation, which gives more sharpness and vigor. A distortion of this would simply be the execution of the leap itself with the oppositional preparation omitted.

In the composition of a dance, WEIDMAN makes intensive use of contrast and variations of intensity. The latter means that differing degrees of two or three specific movements may very easily occupy a whole dance. This should be obvious, but, considering many of today's dancers, it apparently is not. Their compositions are overloaded with so many movements and movement phrases that, as a result, they lose the sense of coherence and unity. The lack of contrast will also produce monotony and incoherence. "One of the most valuable assets in dance composition," he says, "is the formula of contrast. In painting, this formula is made use of in the contrasting of darks against lights, of cool colors against warm ones, of plain surfaces against decorative ones. In movement this is done by contrasting a soft movement against a hard one; the moving of the body or any of its parts from a closed, contracted position to an open, explosive one; or the moving from vertical to horizontal." It gives variety and very often illuminates and vitalizes certain movements that would seem dead without this contrast.

In conclusion, there must be some mention of pantomime. Its dictionary definition, "a series of actions that express meaning without spoken words," is not a satisfactory one because it might apply to many types of dance . . . to the abstract as well as to the personal.

The first distinction that WEIDMAN would make would be the necessity of form. Too often the pantomime or the pantomimic dance depends for its force on the subject matter alone, and whatever formal principles are involved are usually those of the written story. On this background the action is strung along. This process not only weakens the miming, but also does not give full power to the story itself. The first point, then, is that the movement must be developed as a unit, as a logical succession. In composing a pantomimic dance, WEIDMAN uses the same principles he has enunciated for the abstract dance so that, if the story were intelligible, it could nevertheless stand on its own feet.

This does not mean that, with the deletion of the subject matter, the pantomime would automatically become an abstract dance, but it does mean that the approach is so similar that the remainder would be a satisfying formalized design.

This formal development of the action opens many more possibilities. The pantomimic dance, even though brought into dance-form, may still remain extremely literal. Any step beyond this brings it closer and closer to the abstract. Having created specific "subject matter" dances, WEIDMAN has now turned his interest to the point where the pantomime and the abstract intersect. This coincidence of the two in a single dance, when carried to larger dimensions, will very likely characterize what may someday be called the American ballet. Both of these elements have been inherent in the ballets of France and Russia but rarely, if at all, have they fused to create a solid form. Those ballets have usually been an interlarding of the two. WEIDMAN is working consciously toward a fusion so that every movement in itself will contain both.

H O L M

Discussion of what is usually termed "the modern dance" revolves today around the two focal points of American and German interpretations of the art. How often do these discussions reveal any real depth of perception in their easily made comparisons and criticisms? Yet the very fact of their frequent juxtaposition is indicative of the necessity and, I think, of the value of so considering them. Not merely because these two dance cultures are the most recent in their point of expression, nor because of certain slight external similarities are they worthy of analytical comparison, but because they exemplify two constitutionally different responses to identical forces active in the world today.

In America as in Germany, new rhythms, new tempi, shifting tendencies and re-orientation of attitudes in the whole social body are apparent. Many of these changes seem abrupt, but all are traceable in their initial impetus to the period of two or three decades past. The modern dance here and abroad had its inception during this period of change, of readjustment and of frequent upheaval. But while in both countries these developments were concurrent and related to world-wide movements, yet their differences are too significant to permit of sweeping generalizations. The recognition of these common causes of a spiritual kinship in the modern dance is important. But important also is the recognition and understanding of differences and of their implication in the dance. However widely a new dance movement may spread, whatever its common characteristics, there will always be those countless nuances of interpretation, those infinite variations on a ground base inevitable in all the phases of human culture.

79

Like a great river the original source spreads and subdivides, encircling the world in an ever widening network of tributaries—some closely related, others seemingly utterly divorced. The customs, the past history, the present crisis, and the racial and national temperaments all play their part in determining the final result. An organic development of this kind can be sensed, it can be followed, and through inspiration and genius it can be furthered on its way. But it can not be arbitrarily prescribed, nor dare we limit or stem its onrush.

A grasp of at least these essentials is imperative to a sound understanding of the nature of the American dance today. It is an understanding moreover that must not remain merely verbal or theoretical in its manifestations. For the stranger from a European culture the temptation may be to observe rather than to participate, to maintain past achievement and standards at the expense of further progress through absorption and assimilation. The teacher who would approach her work with honesty must keep always pliable in the face of new influences, must be ever ready to learn, to understand as well as to instruct. In undertaking the guidance of each new group there are numerous adjustments to be made by the truly sensitive teacher. How much greater must be the awareness and responsiveness of one who would bring her message, be it small or large of import, to a new country and new people.

The dance, like any cultural expression, when brought from one country to another must undergo some changes. National characteristics and rhythms must be acknowledged and absorbed before any pedagogical method can be considered valid. Gifts must be made with understanding if they are to realize their potentialities as contributions to an art legitimately and without confusion or insincerity. This must be the first principle of the educator. Any attempt to superimpose the externals of method or form must always be unsuccessful and can become positively detrimental in its consequences.

In the interest of this exchange I have based my approach to my American teaching experiences. Soon after the beginning of my work here I found myself moved by certain differences in environment and temperament which came gradually, if not to change, at least to color my former convictions and attitudes. As time passed I have tried to clarify and analyze these differences and to seek for that deeper unity without which the ideals of the dance education as it had been conceived by MARY WIGMAN could have no real part in the field of the American dance. Perhaps the first conclusion to be made by a European observer is the vast difference in the present stages of Continental and American cultures with all that their respective age and youth alone imply. The difficulties in the way of the development of an indigenous American culture have been manifold. In the first place her material growth during her comparatively brief history has been so phenomenal as to force all else into the background of the national consciousness. First a new country to be explored and settled, a country of vast proportions and in an absolutely virgin state, and subsequently the development of the tremendous natural resources over great distances—this left little time or energy to be devoted to any but the most practical of the arts. And having established an initial momentum, the industrial fields reached and surpassed in a few decades what had taken centuries in even the leading European nations.

The achievement of this international pre-eminence in the mechanical and industrial fields obviously made incongruous the crude state of the native folk arts. The natural result was to turn the attention to those European countries where time and a more uniform rate of progress had allowed the growth and flowering of a mature and firmly grounded art. Music and painting, literature

81

and foreign arts and crafts were imported to adorn the homes, and to entertain the leisure moments of the well-to-do. The American artist in his formative stage was either ignored or disparaged, or forced to model his work after established European traditions. The general trend became more cosmopolitan and urban than national in the true sense of the word. This state of development cannot be criticized—it was an inevitable outcome of other forces which were not to be denied.

Today there has been an awakening to the work of folk tradition, a search for native sources in theme, medium and form. With this awakening of the American consciousness to its own inherent and unexplored fields, the artist is given that help and freedom so necessary in the building of a foundation for a truly American art. Still, the tradition of quick results and success that has been won in industrial fields is not easily forgotten. Results, even today, are the standard of measure—as, in the ultimate reckoning, is only right. But their importance should not be allowed to obscure entirely the values of the states of development, even of the occasional failures, necessary in the gradual unfolding of the artist's powers toward maturity. This sense of tolerance, of patience and of interest, even for the slow and perhaps awkward early steps of the artist is one of the contributions of the European attitude.

America, because of her youth, is sometimes too quick to assume the outward forms of any new and striking foreign products: to admire, and immediately to accept, without assimilating their true qualities, new modes for their novelty alone. These fads, phenomenal in their appeal at the moment, are soon forgotten for more recent novelties with none of their potential contributions realized. In connection with the contemporary German dance, for example, there have been those who after a brief course of study at one of the

German schools of the dance have returned to this country to teach as a new gospel the superficial forms which they have selected from a wide and frequently difficult field. This is unfair both to the German and to the American dancer or teacher who views her work with a sense of responsibility. Whatever gains can be made—and there are great possibilities—can be made only in a spirit of mutual co-operation and exchange.

The entire orientation of the dance of MARY WIGMAN is towards the establishment of a relationship between man and his universe. It is this philosophical tendency that influences the emotional, spatial, and functional aspects of her own dancing and likewise her pedagogical principles. Emotionally the German dance is basically subjective and the American dance objective in their characteristic manifestations. This is of course a generalization and as such true only to the point of exceptions, but I believe it throws some light on their fundamental emotional departure. The tendency of the American dancer is to observe, portray and comment on her surroundings with an insight lighted mainly by intellectual comprehension and analysis. This applies to the foremost and most recent examples in this country. Up until the present the trend was toward either the purely pictorial and decorative or the predominately functional.

The German dancer on the other hand starts with the actual emotional experience itself and its effect upon the individual. The distinction is one of "being" as contrasted with "doing"—of immersing the self in an emotional state as the necessary prelude to creation as contrasted with objective reconstruction of a known situation. Each of these approaches have their potential weaknesses and individual strengths. In the American method there is a danger of straying so far from the source in its reality that the final product loses in warmth and communicable fervor whatever it may have gained in perception.

In the German dance there is inherent the dangers of looseness of form, obscurity, and the attendant evils of mere self-expressionism. Properly controlled, however, and disciplined within its medium, this approach lends depth, radiance, and emotional conviction to the dancer's effort. Properly disciplined, I believe that the awakening and stimulation of confidence in instinct and emotion can be a valuable contribution to the education of the American dancer. The German pedagogical technique employs for this end improvisation on emotional as well as functional themes aimed first at freedom of expression but ultimately toward integrated composition. Without form we cannot speak of art, but the form must be an integer, not a superimposed part of the whole and must glow unmistakably with that inner flame which is its source and its significance.

This subjective and emotional approach colors even more subtly the use of space characteristic of the German dancer, it accounts at least in part for the greater consciousness of space, actual and created, as a factor of tremendous importance. Space, rhythm, volume, proportion are realized both by the American and the German dancer of first rank. But the use of space as an emotional element, an active partner in the dance, is distinctly European. Possibly because of a past more complex and a destiny more at the mercy of outer forces than is the case in America, we have become aware of the dramatic implications in the vision of the individual pitted against the universe. Space, with its constrictions and its immensity, its dark vistas and blinding horizons, becomes for the dancer an invitation or a menace, but in any case, an inescapable element. The American dancer seems frequently to have little use, to be but slightly aware of space except as an incidental factor in design and floor pattern. Perhaps it is because the American background has had no external obstructions to their conquest of the vastnesses of their continent, because distances have succumbed with relatively little struggle to the pioneer's onward march, that the American dancer stands above and so often untouched by space as an active agent. MARY WIGMAN, from whose genius and early experiments the entire German dance derived its present standing, illustrates perfectly this intimate feeling for space. Those of us who worked with her at the start of her career will be forever permeated with those fundamental principles toward which she has always striven. In the realm of space particularly, I feel that MARY WIGMAN has made a great contribution to the contemporary dance. In her dances she alternately grapples with space as an opponent and caresses it as though it were a living, sentient thing. In her gestures and movements she carves boldly and delicately visible and fluid forms, shaping, surrounding, and sinking in the space which presses close about her.

Similarly, this emotional impetus makes felt its influence even in the physical techniques of the moving body. Superb and precise as is the technical virtuosity of even the less than great American dancers, their approach and interest are usually directed toward bodily accomplishment for its own sake. Even though a given dance may be composed to convey an emotional theme the mechanics used in its externalization are separately developed. A gesture and movement vocabulary are first prepared and only subsequently employed in various combinations for various ends. This can be done with finished and brilliant results, but it is an approach radically different from that of the German dancer. For us each composition evolves through its own emotional demands, not only its special gestures, but more important still, its particular tension and even its distinctive technique. Naturally the preliminary training of the dancer is based upon a physical as well as an emotional development but its scope is general rather than specific in aim. The functions of the moving body, moreover,

"ecstatic experience creates its own forms" — Betty Lind

are felt rather than visualized and the whole being encouraged to participate rather than merely to direct. Particularly indicative of this tendency is the use of what we have called "states" of movement as an instrument for emotional freedom and enlarged and revitalized horizons in movement concepts.

These principles which are incorporated in the educational method of MARY WIGMAN have, I believe, much that will be worthwhile to the American dancer. Through her the existence and importance of the eternal source of dancing—sensed by many others at this time—is made articulate. Realizing the error and futility of teaching dance forms in themselves, her credo leaves open all question of personal or national systems and results, and is content to point out the underground springs that wait to be tapped by the individual artist. In America, more perhaps than anywhere else in the world today, there waits fresh and vigorous material for the dance. In its environment and in the temperament and vitality of its people the future American dance has an enviable heritage.

S T E W A R T

When Isadora Duncan lived, she said, "I believe that my school will create a new art or show the way toward it. Only the new generation will be able to express the new world and find new genius and new ideas."

Isadora died disappointed, but unknowingly she left behind her a new generation creating a new art of the dance, a new generation fighting, also, as Isadora fought, for new ideas, for the recognition of new genius, the recognition of the young dancers who believe that their dance is a sincere expression of their generation, a generation desiring freedom. The spiritual leader of this new generation was and still is Mary Wigman, for whom America and Germany have the highest regard and admiration.

Just as Isadora Duncan did before her, so does Mary Wigman leave a trail of glory behind her after every recital, on either side of which (in America at least) lies an opposing camp. Mary is amused. So was Isadora. There are always those who understand and appreciate what genius is saying, and there are always those who never can understand, and who persist in finding some characteristic of the dancer to use as an object of scorn. Thus it always has been and doubtless always will be as long as there are men and women of genius working out their ideas.

But regardless of the scorn, they go on working and the world comes to realize that art is changing and that those things recently thought to be amusingly ultra-modern are being accepted as a matter of course. And so it is . . . a matter of course.

Among those who accepted ISADORA's dance philosophy and that of MARY WIGMAN, there are two types of followers: those who are content to copy the outward form, and those who attempt to understand the ideal behind the form and proceed from that to their own individual expression.

Strangely enough, the pedagogics of both ISADORA DUNCAN and of MARY WIGMAN are not written down into a system or method. At least the two great dancers have never written them down nor suggested that any one else do so. They have believed that each student, in his own individual manner, comes to a realization of what the dance means and of what the movement of the human body may express.

The modern dance was born when ISADORA DUNCAN, the great American-born dancer, exerted the effort of will necessary to overthrow the superficial forms of the traditional ballet and to dance what she personally felt as a human being. So too, MARY WIGMAN believes that the source of the dance is in the basic human emotions. All sincere, true, genuine movements in the dance will be the dancer's own individual expressions of those basic emotions that belong to the whole of humanity. If the dance springs from this source in a unified form, the audience will experience with the dancer the same emotions that are being expressed through movement. If a dance, created out of the dancer's experience of life is thus given, the movement and its inherent emotion will go from the dancer's body through the audience, and perhaps . . . like music when a tone is struck . . . on into infinity, from whence it may return in changed form to the dancer to refill that mysteriously ever-flowing well which is the source of all movement. The more the dancer gives of herself, the more she has to give.

There should be no lamentation over the death of dances when their creator dies, for those dances are so very closely of and by the body and soul of the dancer that their repetition by another person would be but meaningless mimicry. WIGMAN's greatest aspiration is that young dancers will be so moved by her dances, which are personal expressions of humanity, that each will continue the effervescent creation of the real dance from his own body and soul. It is the dance of life!

Although the emotion expressed may be one which has been felt by every human being from the beginning up to the present, the body movement, the expression, must spring out of today's life and be felt by today's audience.

The modern dance springs out of the very heart of man. It goes back to the source of human life. It throws away superficiality and moves out into the open spaces where abide the heart and soul of mankind. In this marvelous harmony of oneness with the great things of nature, the body and soul come into unity with the cosmos.

In music, the masterpieces of yesterday can be seen and heard again. They can be used as models and as sources of inspiration in the creating of music today. Dancing is different. It remains only in the memory. After a dancer and his dances are gone they can never be seen nor felt again. Therefore, each new dancer must discover for himself and out of his very self, the art of the dance.

The dancer is under obligation to his fellow men to create in expressive, meaningful movement, those feelings in himself which are also in the heart and soul of every living human being.

Such is the dancer's responsibility.

ARMITAGE

Modern dance is an independent art of the stage, related to all dance forms which have preceded it, but more particularly to other art forms contemporaneous with it. In varying degrees the qualities of condensation, economy, and elimination are the essence of all contemporary expression.

It is impossible for the creative artist to be uninfluenced by conditions and the world which surrounds him.

Condensation, economy, and elimination are basic in the work of Schoenberg, Hindemuth and in all compositions of Stravinsky succeeding "La Sacre du Printemps."

It is particularly dominant among creative painters. In the work of Klee, Picasso, Kandinsky, three of the most significant men of our time, the most casual survey will disclose the successful attempt to reduce statements in paint to their most revealing essence. It is interesting in passing to draw attention to the parallel between the work of the painter Kandinsky, and the composer Stravinsky. Both have had their explosive kaleidoscopic periods. Both have inevitably drawn near the monochromatic ideal. The "Duo" of Stravinsky and the "White Soft and Hard" of Kandinsky have a striking aesthetic relationship as well as a relationship of form.

Sculpture travels in the same direction. Brancusi was probably the first to discover that condensation, economy and elimination enhanced the tension and the force of his forms, and from this has developed his aesthetic philosophy. Practically without exception are the significant contemporary sculptors working towards this end, a fine example being the work of Moore. It is practiced by even the more conventional men, such as Maillol and Epstein. Lembruch understood it.

Condensation, economy, and elimination are the underlying motivations in modern architecture, and are the very core of functionalism. Beginning with Sullivan, it continues through Frank Lloyd Wright, in the work of Le Courbusier, Lescaze and many other architects in Europe and America. The whole tendency has been and is towards a utilitarian employment of these objectives. Whether or not this is come about by intellectualized intention or whether it has come as a functional necessity is unimportant. It is the contemporary direction and it is wedded happily to a new sense of freedom and a new discipline.

It is not deriding the dance of other periods when we say that modern exponents have been the first to free this art form from allegory and literature. No significant work and no great art needs to be a synthesis of several arts. Just as contemporary painting has thrown off the handicap of painting representational subject matter, and just as music has become "pure music" and not a means of manifesting commonplace human emotions, the dance has entered a newer, possibly higher, certainly a greater sphere.

In America there has been much external searching for something nationalistic among the less imaginative and uncreative artists in all fields. There has been, among dancers, a great deal of energy expended in imitation of skyscrapers, airplanes, and the objective mechanics of today. In paint, Grant Wood, Thomas Benton, and Curry of Kansas have been leaders in the "American Scene" school. Neither the painters nor the dancers have found anything characteristically American in this adolescent approach. They have succeeded only in superimposing European influences.

Developing out of conflicting aims and indecisiveness is a dance, which, because it is simple and direct, has many of the virtues which we like to consider American. It has indeed qualities not found elsewhere. But even this new forthrightness, as distinctly American as it is, cannot be completely detached nor unrelated.

Certain critics believe that the American dancer has been inclined to overestimate the importance of his contribution and his actual achievement. If the American dancer needs a defense, he has an ample one in the obstructions he has had to surmount and the romantic prejudice he has had to face. He has had to overcome a public steeped in the traditions of crinoline. Another quality which has been a barrier is the undisputable fact that much Modern Dance is for the performer rather than the audience, and that certain laboratory experiments have been made on the stage which should have taken place in the studio.

This book has a value over and above any literary brilliance or limitation, because it sets forth in the performer's or creator's own words the story of his or her approach.

To their testimony I should like to add a statement made by Kurt Jooss: "Every member of my troup is an actor as well as a dancer, and must be skilled in expressing the gamut of emotions by extreme simplicity of means."

The modern dancer, then, has discovered that as he moves in the direction of simplicity, he approaches certain geometric forms, known also to the modern painter, sculptor and composer. He reacts to them because they symbolize the universal analogy in all formal relations.

PART III
BIOGRAPHIES

A R T U R   M I C H E L

Dr. Artur Michel, well-known as one of the most outstanding dance critics in Germany, first became interested in the dance through his study of rhythm in the universities where he was specializing in the history of European literature. From his work on an essay investigating the rhythm of Goethe's poems, he was led to study the rhythm of music and the dance. His first critique on the latter was written in 1919, the same year in which Mary Wigman gave her first dance recital in Berlin. Since 1922, he has been dance and theatre critic of the *Berlin Vossische Zeitung*.

M A R Y   W I G M A N

MARY WIGMAN was born in Hanover, Germany, where she attended the high school for girls and studied voice and piano. Later she studied in England and French-Switzerland and in 1911 she became a student at the famous Dalcroze School in Hellerau. After receiving her diploma she continued her study of the dance with RUDOLPH VON LABAN in Munich and Zurich. In 1919 MARY WIGMAN gave her first performances in Germany and Switzerland. In 1920 she founded her school in Dresden which later became the Central Institute of all WIGMAN Schools. In the years following, MARY WIGMAN appeared with a chamber dance group, creating the group dances "Fairy Tale", "Dance Macabre", "Songs of Space" and "The Festival." She concerned herself with the completion of her pedagogical work, the founding of branch institutes and courses and the spreading of dance consciousness. To her solo tours through the principal cities of Europe were added two tours of the United States in 1930 and in 1931 when she performed the cycles "Shifting Landscape" and "Sacrifice." In 1932-33 she presented the group-dance "The Way" in both Germany and America. During the season of 1933-34 MARY WIGMAN gave forty solo recitals in Germany and other European countries. The programs of this tour included a new suite of two dances called "Frauentanze" (Dances of Women). During the 1934-35 season MARY WIGMAN and her new group danced in Berlin in the 1934 Reich Festival for Dance held in December. After the Festival MARY WIGMAN and her group toured Germany and other European countries.

There have been three books published concerning MARY WIGMAN: *Das Mary Wigman Werk*, by RUDOLPH BACH; *Mary Wigman*, by RUDOLPH VON DELIUS, and *Die Verwandlungen der Mary Wigman*, by KURT LINDER.

P A L U C C A

PALUCCA, although born in Bavaria, spent her childhood in California. She returned to Germany, however, where she started to study dancing at the age of fifteen. She worked for two years with balletmaster Kroller of the Munich state-opera, after which she became a member of MARY WIGMAN's first group of pupils in Dresden. She remained with this group until 1923, when her own artistic career as a concert dancer began. Since then, tours have been arranged for her in Germany and other European countries. In 1925, the PALUCCA School in Dresden was founded, having since produced many solo and stage dancers as well as teachers of the dance. The courses given include solo and group stage-dancing, rhythmics, gymnastics, pedagogics and others. The PALUCCA dance-group and dance-trio were formed from the most talented pupils. In 1933, the Nerthus Picture Corporation filmed the first dance picture from the dance "Serenata," one of PALUCCA's finest creations. In the 1934 German Dance Festival, PALUCCA appeared as solo dancer, and as director of a small group from her school.

HARALD KREUTZBERG

HARALD KREUTZBERG was born in Reichenberg, a small town in German Bohemia. His grandfather was director of a large travelling circus and later made and exhibited wax figures in Europe and America. KREUTZBERG's father was born in Philadelphia while the grandfather was exhibiting there. From his grandfather HARALD KREUTZBERG inherited a love for the theatrical world. As a child he showed talent for music, painting and dancing. His greatest desire was to enter the theater, and so he was occasionally allowed to take children's parts on the stage. As a young man he moved with his parents to Dresden where he studied painting and costume designing in the Art Academy. At the same time he studied dancing in the Mary Wigman School in Dresden where he gained the fundamentals of his dance work. MAX TERPIS, who was also a student in the Wigman School at that time, became balletmaster at the Hannover Opera. KREUTZBERG joined him there to study and to dance in the chorus. After one year in Hannover, TERPIS and KREUTZBERG went to Berlin where TERPIS was now balletmaster of the Staatsoper. KREUTZBERG stayed three years in Berlin during which time he danced the "Jester" part in a very successful opera, "Don Morte," by WILKENS. Since this ballet in Berlin FRIEDRICH WILCKENS has been KREUTZBERG's accompanist and composer. MAX REINHARDT saw KREUTZBERG in Berlin and invited him to Salzburg where he first danced the "Master of Ceremonies," in GOZZI's "Turandot." After the first summer in Salzburg, KREUTZBERG went with REINHARDT to America where he took the part of "Puck" in "Midsummer's Night Dream." While in New York KREUTZBERG gave a dance recital with TILLY LOSCH from the Vienna Opera who was also in the REINHARDT group. KREUTZBERG returned to Europe and danced in the ballets of the Leipsig Opera and with YVONNE GEORGI at the Hannover Opera. The following three seasons KREUTZBERG and GEORGI toured the United States. In 1931-32 KREUTZBERG toured with his own group, the following year alone, in 1933-34 with RUTH PAGE of the Chicago Opera, adding the Orient to that year's tour, and in 1934-35 after participation in the German Dance Festival as a solo dancer, he toured Central Europe and Eastern United States.

Two books have been published concerning HARALD KREUTZBERG:— *Harald Kreutzberg und Yvonne Georgi*, by DR. WILLE, and *Der Tanzer, Harald Kreutzberg*, by HELENE VON TAUSSIG; the latter book contains 24 dance sketches by HELENE VON TAUSSIG, and published by the Mozartium Academy of Salzburg.

HANNS HASTING

Before becoming permanently connected in 1929 with the Wigman School as pianist-composer, HANNS HASTING had done considerable work in connection with the modern dance, since 1925. Having studied music in Holland, Dresden and Berlin since he was eight years old, he had a thorough background for the position which he held in 1928 as musical director of the Berlin Wigman School. During the next year, he toured Europe with MARY WIGMAN, directing the dance orchestra for the performances of "Totenmal" during the Munich Festival. He has accompanied her on three tours of the United States and several tours of Central Europe; also giving lectures and having articles published in both Europe and America on the relationship of music and the dance, the subject in which he is especially interested. MR. HASTING has composed the music for MARY WIGMAN's four great cycles, "Shifting Landscape," "Sacrifice," "The Way," and "Dances of Women," as well as many compositions played at special recitals and dance concerts. In 1934 MR. HASTING accompanied MARY WIGMAN and her group in the "Dances of Women" cycle, and the small group dances given in the German Dance Festival and the European tour which followed.

P A U L   L O V E

After graduating from Princeton University with a Bachelor of Arts degree, PAUL LOVE became dance editor of the Theatre Guild Magazine. Later he was one of the inaugural editors of the *Dance Observer* magazine which first appeared in February, 1934. At various times he has contributed articles to *Modern Music Quarterly* and *Trend Magazine* and has done free-lance drawing for the *Theatre Guild Magazine* and *The Forum*. In 1935 MR. LOVE was general manager and a member of the audition board of the Modern Dance Recital Course given at the New School for Social Research in New York City.

MARTHA GRAHAM

MARTHA GRAHAM, a tenth generation American, was born in Pittsburgh. She is a direct descendant of MILES STANDISH. She lived in Pittsburgh until she was ten, when her father, a well known physician, moved his family to Santa Barbara, California. She was educated in private schools in Santa Barbara and Los Angeles. MARTHA GRAHAM did not study dancing until she was in her third year in high school, although she can not remember the time when it was not her wish to be a dancer. When she was 16 years old she saw a dance concert by RUTH ST. DENIS, and her desire to dance was crystallized. In the summer of that year, 1916, she went to Los Angeles to study at the Denishawn School. In 1919 she returned to the Denishawn School as a student teacher. Following this she was soloist with the Denishawn Concert Company. 1924-25 she taught at Eastman School of Music in Rochester. She made her New York debut in recital in 1926. Her subsequent activities include: Dancing leading role in STRAUSS' *Heldenleben*, with the Cleveland Orchestra under SOKOLEFF; LOEFFLER's *Pagan Poem* also with the Cleveland Orchestra, both of which were IRENE LEWISOHN's productions. In 1930 she did STRAVINSKY's *Sacre du Printemps*, with the Philadelphia Orchestra under the direction of STOKOWSKI. In 1932 was awarded a Guggenheim Fellowship. Directed Stage Alliance's production of *Six Miracle Plays* in 1933, and assisted in the direction of action in KATHERINE CORNELL's production of *Lucrece*. Subsequently, directed action for ARCHIBALD McLEISH's *Panic* and Choreography for *Panorama*. Has given more than fifty recitals in New York City since 1926, in addition to tours. On staffs of Neighborhood Playhouse Studios, Bennington School of the Dance, and is Chairman of Dance Division of Mayor LaGuardia's Municipal Art Committee.

D O R I S   H U M P H R E Y

After studying the ballet for a short time, DORIS HUMPHREY taught and danced in the Denishawn group for about ten years. In 1928, having new ideas of her own she started a school and gave her first New York recital with CHARLES WEIDMAN. Her success was so immediate that, during the following years, she appeared with the Cleveland Orchestra, with the Neighborhood Playhouse, with the Philadelphia Symphony Orchestra, and with the Philharmonic, in addition to individual concert recitals and teaching in her own school and at the New School for Social Research and the Dalton School. Her best known compositions for Group are "The Water Study," "Life of the Bee," "The Shakers," "Dionysiaques." Her largest single work, the "Orestes" of Milhaud has not yet been produced. In 1932 she choreographed many of the dances for the revue "Americana," and arranged the ritual movement in "Run Little Chillun." She appeared in the Theatre Guilds, "School for Husbands" in 1933 and choreographed the ballet interlude. With CHARLES WEIDMAN she created the dances and danced in the 1935 production of "Iphigenia" with the Philadelphia Symphony and Opera Association.

CHARLES WEIDMAN

CHARLES WEIDMAN received his initial training in the dance at the Denishawn School and toured the Orient with the Denishawn group. In 1928, he started a school of his own in conjunction with DORIS HUMPHREY. In addition to his teaching and concert work, both solo and with groups of men, he has presented two major ballets, "Candide" and "The Happy Hypocrite." He has done the choreography and danced in the operas presented by the Cleveland Orchestra, appeared in productions of the Neighborhood Playhouse, and danced with the Philadelphia and Philharmonic Symphony Orchestras. He has choreographed dances for "Americana", "Hold Your Horses", "Flying Colors", "As Thousands Cheer," and "Life Begins at 8:40," and created and danced his own part in the Theatre Guild's "School for Husbands" and recently with DORIS HUMPHREY created the dances and danced in the Philadelphia Symphony Orchestra's opera production of "Iphigenia."

H A N Y A H O L M

HANYA HOLM, director and chief teacher of the only official Wigman School of the Dance in America, is a recognized authority on the pedagogy and educational aspects of the Wigman approach. As a young teacher of the Dalcroze method, HANYA HOLM saw the early recitals of MARY WIGMAN, and soon after became one of the first students of her school. After studying intensively with MARY WIGMAN, she became a member of the Wigman Concert Group, and also a teacher and member of the board of directors of the Wigman Central Institute, Dresden. In addition to her activities as dancer and teacher, MISS HOLM has served as dance director for two summer seasons at Omnen, Holland, and as co-director and dancer with MARY WIGMAN in ALBERT TALHOFF's "Das Totenmal." Responding to the popular demand for a school founded on her principles, MARY WIGMAN decided to open an American branch of the Dresden Institute. HANYA HOLM was chosen to represent her in this country. Since her arrival in America, MISS HOLM has written and lectured extensively in educational fields, and has given courses in several of the summer dance centers connected with certain American colleges.

ACKNOWLEDGMENTS

The publishers are indebted to RAMIEL MCGEHEE, who edited this entire book; to FRANZISKA BOAS for translations, and to the photographers EDWARD WESTON, SOICHI SUNAMI, BEN PINCHOT, CH. RUDOLPH, MARCUS BLECHMAN and H. HEWETT, for portraits and groups reproduced.